Also by Baron Perlman

Come Collect With Me:
Musings on Collecting and
American Antiques

THE COLLECTOR'S WORLD

More Musings on Collecting
and American Antiques

Baron Perlman

CKBooks Publishing

No part of this book can be used or reproduced in any manner without the consent of the author except in the case of brief quotations for reviews. Contact the author at comecollectwithme.com

Publisher's Cataloging-in-Publication Data
Names: Perlman, Baron, author.
Title: The collector's world : more musings on collecting and American antiques / Baron Perlman.
Description: New Glarus, WI : CKBooks Publishing, 2021 | Includes index.
Identifiers: ISBN 978-1-949085-51-8 (paperback) | ISBN 978-1-949085-52-5 (hardcover) | ISBN 978-1-949085-53-2 (ebook)
Subjects: LCSH: Antiques--United States. | Collectors and collecting--United States. | Decorative arts--Collectors and collecting--United States. | Antiques--Psychological aspects. | BISAC: ANTIQUES & COLLECTIBLES / General.
Classification: LCC NK1125 .P433 2021 (print) | LCC NK1125 (ebook) | DDC 745.1--dc23.

LCCN: 2021924160

Copyright 2021 by Baron Perlman
All rights reserved

CKBooks Publishing
P.O. Box 214
New Glarus, WI
53574
ckbookspublishing.com

To my wife, Sandy
~ Collector Extraordinaire ~

Table of Contents

Foreword ix
Acknowledgements xi
Preface xiii
Introduction xiv
The Collector's World xviii

Section I • A Plethora of Feelings:
        What Collectors Experience and Why
Chapter 1 - Anticipation 1
Chapter 2 - A Collector's Concerns 7
Chapter 3 - Courage 14
Chapter 4 - Disappointment 21
Chapter 5 - Hope 27
Chapter 6 - Nostalgia 33
Chapter 7 - Passion 40
Chapter 8 - Sentimentality 46
Chapter 9 - Trust (Faith) and the American Antique World 52

Section II • A Tasteful Indulgence (Most of the Time)
Chapter 10 - Color 59
Chapter 11 - Condition 66
Chapter 12 - The Psychology of a Well-Designed Show Booth 73
Chapter 13 - The Realm of Rejected Values
        and Bad Behavior by Collectors (and others) 81

Section III • Self-Reflection Isn't Just for Self
Chapter 14 - American Antiques are a Window to
        Our Nation's Past, Present and Future 89
Chapter 15 - Collectors' Angst: What Will We Do
        with Our Collections? 93
Chapter 16 - The Frenzy for Fresh to the Market 99
Chapter 17 - Mine 105

Chapter 18 - Notes on a Pandemic: What I Will Never
          Again Take for Granted..111
Chapter 19 - Occam's Razor: Collector Happiness
          or Fulfillment 117
Chapter 20 - Too Much Stuff 123
Chapter 21 - The Fascination With "Top Sellers" 129

Section IV • Lessons (Sometimes Waiting to Be Learned)
Chapter 22 - Auctions and Collectors: The Psychology of Our
          Bidding (Often More Than We Had Planned) 134
Chapter 23 - Choice 141
Chapter 24 - The Importance of the Word "Important"..............147
Chapter 25 - The Prime Directive: Be Prepared 154
Chapter 26 - Surrounded by One's Collection or Not.................161
Chapter 27 - Three Ghosts of Purchasing Antiques....................167
Chapter 28 - A Timed Auction 173
Chapter 29 - Using Style and Connoisseurship Criteria
          to Buy the Best We Can Afford..............................179
Chapter 30 - The Virtues of Patience 185

Section V • A Wish or Two and Ending With Praise
Chapter 31 - An American Antique Critic..................................193
Chapter 32 - The American Antique Market..............................198
Chapter 33 - A Paean for American Antique Dealers 204
Index 210
About the Author..217

Foreword

The aficionado of antiques is a unique breed: focused, neurotic, lustful, impulsive. At the Thanksgiving table of the family that defines itself as antiques folk, the dealer is the drunken uncle with some controversial and possibly even outdated world views to share – all of which he is absolutely certain he is right about.

I am an antiques dealer, and such was my attitude upon beginning reading Barry Perlman's first book about the niche world I inhabit. In *Come Collect With Me*, I expected to enjoy the different perspectives on a number of age-old subjects that inevitably stretch quick post-auction dinners at the bar into four-hour dissertations. This expectation was satisfied, but Barry's background in psychology and the way he applied it to the topics and character types I live around was a revelation.

Dealers bemoaning the effects of the Internet, an alleged recession, or whatever the latest downer may be often mutter, "Nobody *needs* this stuff." So it was a tremendous revelation for me to learn from Barry that those dealers are wrong. Collectors *do* need to collect. Eureka, salvation! I have always counted myself among the dealers who pursued antiques because they loved them. Yet this revelation made antiques dealing an even more noble pursuit. To spread the gospel of old stuff is a high calling indeed, but to actually help people lead more fulfilling and enriched lives? This was life-changing stuff.

One would think that Barry's soothing words have made the rounds by now – squashing out the general air of malaise which had become pervasive in the antiques world. Collecting is something eternal, it comes in cycles and fads, but it does not die out. Nay, the aficionado of antiques is another thing: stubborn. Yet, Barry persists.

I treasure my friendship with the author. The love of old things seems to be a trait which, when present, consumes the personality and ties like-minded individuals tightly into a community. Many of us are committed to the cause, but Barry rates highly in tenacity, ability, and generosity. The world of antiques can be a nurturing one, but it is also cut-throat. For proof of the culture's selfishness, consider the absence of material written by dealers or collectors to encourage others. It is only natural, collecting can lead to feelings of obsessiveness and paranoia – both lessons I learned from Barry, though not from his example.

The writings contained in this volume and its predecessor represent one of the most valuable tools that exist for collecting and collectors. To my knowledge it is practically unique. It is difficult enough to coerce dealers into writing frankly about the profession, but they do occasionally retire and thus have little to lose by sharing their secrets. For the collector, that one great rarity that has eluded them may appear on the market tomorrow, and if their competition has been clued in to their methodology, it could cost them the prize.

Enjoy the conversations and study the lessons contained here. Collecting is a wonderful journey. If this is your first leg of the trip, you could have no better navigator than Barry. If you are an old salt, prepare for revelations about yourself and your fellow inhabitants in the vast quirky galaxy of collecting antiques.

John Chaski
Camden, Delaware

Acknowledgements

The decision to follow up on my first volume (Come Collect with Me, 2019) was mine but not made alone. In part, because of that book I became friends with collectors, dealers, and auctioneers, some from far away – Noel and Ton in Houston, Jim in Kansas City, Helaine in New York City, Shirley in Indianapolis, John in Delaware, Andrew in Maine. They were supportive of my continued exploration of the collector's world.

I also continued to contribute to *Maine Antique Digest*. If nothing else, letters to the editor in response to my columns told me that the American antique community wanted a chance to explore new ideas. Ten chapters in *The Collector's World* originally appeared there (1, 3, 5, 7, 10, 13, 15, 16, 18, 25).

I did not pound my keyboard in isolation. Clayton Pennington, Editor of *Maine Antique Digest* encouraged me. My dear friend, Tom Herzing suggested I take my ideas and put them together in this tome. He also repeatedly urged me to write clearly, to have fun in my writing, to avoid being dull, and of course he never hesitated to tell me what failed to meet the rudimentary standards of clarity.

Collectors responding to my monthly blog at Comecollectwithme.com gave me support, ideas, and most of all inspiration. "What about . . .?" is the eternal, nagging question that inspires authors.

In reaching out to the American antique community I received more assistance than I expected and perhaps deserved. John Chaski, dealer and a collector of all things Delaware told me when I was "right on" and far off. David Schorsch in a lengthy phone conversation told stories of the characters in the antique collecting business from long ago. Andrew Davis educated me regarding the auction world. Other dealers, some with high standards and who seldom gave praise (I was told by others) wrote that they had enjoyed a *MAD* column.

I thank Athena Rylance, granddaughter of dear friends, the artist who provided this book's delightful cover painting. Talent at an early age is a blessing, one that deserves to be acknowledged and encouraged.

Finally, I must admit the value of my wife Sandy's patience, encouragement, and good sense. A wise and talented woman, she keeps our home full of American antiques sane and beautiful, and she even tolerates my hiding upstairs, scribbling away.

I continued to think of myself as a fledging author sending his fragile creation into a chaotic, thankless world. Once again, as I did with *Come Collect with Me*, I repeat Chaucer's entreaty, "go lyttle booke." I hope it is received with the spirit I intended: as a gift to collectors.

Barry Perlman
Oshkosh, Wisconsin
2021

Preface

Collecting is an extraordinary thing. At its most basic, it is mere accumulation, a piling up. Misers do that with money. Dictators do that with conquests. Pack rats do it with everything from cigar wrappers to shiny pebbles.

Then a particularly human presence enters the scene: taste, aesthetics, the appreciation of the beautiful, the well-crafted, the rare – it goes by many names. But add the two together and you end up with wonders like the Louvre's exhibits, Phidias' sculptures – and, yes, antique collections.

You will note that I did not hesitate to use the word <u>human</u> in composing that bold assertion. True, pack rats do "collect," but as far as we know, it has nothing to do with appreciation, understanding, cogitation, ambition, or intent. What particularly interests me is the intersection between the psychology of human beings and their actions in the world of antique collecting. What is the drive that makes studying, preserving, and appreciating the past glories of American craftsmanship – broadly defined – attractive for some and not others? What are the habits, distractions and mistakes collectors make, and why? What is the actual geography of the collector's world?

I have tried probing these questions for years, sometimes reflecting on my own behavior and errors, sometimes providing an objective critique, almost always offering opinions (and I hope insights). As time has passed, I have become sensitized to the psychological forces that drive antique collecting. What follows is a deep plunge into the hobby . . . and the minds and feelings of those who share my passion.

Introduction

The pandemic gave me ample time for reflection and long stretches in which to write. I was surprised at the many nuances involved in collecting and was struck by the hobby's vital importance in the lives of those who collect American antiques (as my wife and I do).

With my background as a psychologist and my history as a long-time collector, I am well versed and respectful of the powerful place feelings play in a person's life. This book opens with an assessment of the feelings and needs that a collector endures – hope, concern, disappointment, anticipation, passion, courage, sentimentality, nostalgia, and trust (faith). These feelings offer a glimpse at the inner world of a collector and the forces that motivate his behavior. The observant reader will notice there is no chapter devoted to love. Instead, I think of this book as one long collector's love story.

I thought of what enticed me, what I looked for in the objects I collected, and how they related to my eye and pocketbook. Out of them arose such musings as booth designs at an antique show or of the importance of color and the condition in the objects we look at, desire, and purchase. But as in any realm of our lives, all is not ideal. Collectors are no different from the ordinary run of humanity in their misbehaving. Having read two detective stories that took place in hell, I used the netherworld as my setting for collector sins and loss of virtue.

Sitting on our couch as the days passed, I thought about what American antiques can teach us about history. I am aging and I was facing with a problem with no clear solution. What to do with our collection some day. I also knew that collectors can be less than rational, whipped to a feverish pitch by items fresh to the market. A recent book, *Mine*, gave me a fresh perspective on what I owned and what it actually meant to own something. The pandemic was devastating to me as a collector because of a loss of personal contact with people, though it led me to treasure them more than ever. I adopted Occom's Razor paring collecting to its bare bones and the column on happiness and fulfillment was born. Because our house is full (as is the case for many collectors), I wondered, can one ever own too much stuff? And what is a collector's fascination with the most expensive pieces anyway?

Eventually I got to the bare soul of collecting. I call it Lessons (Sometimes Waiting to be Learned). Auctions, curse them or love them had to be discussed. Harking back to my liberal arts education so long ago, I had to confront myself as a choosing entity. The spending of money is manipulated less by things than by words, hence the importance of the word important to collectors. The critical collector's maxim "be prepared" was inspected as was another prime directive, the development and use of appropriate style and connoisseurship criteria when collecting. What one collects even determines whether one lives with the treasures in plain sight or packed away. Finally, issues of patience slid under the microscope.

The book's last section contains two if-I-were-king-for-a-day chapters. I yearn for the eruption of a dominant American antique critic. I tried (and probably only partially succeeded) to describe the American antique market and ended up hoping perhaps one day better data will exist. Finally, I felt that dealers were too important to only be referred to now and again, and so I penned a paean for them.

I mention here and there that I have written about a topic previously, *Come Collect with Me* (2019). The present chapters are new and were put together over three years.

What I write about collecting American antiques applies to those who collect all sorts of things. For some, finding items is easier, for others for difficult. For some, the prices are less, for others, pieces cost more. But to be a collector is to share a world with others, regardless of what they bring home, live with or display.

All this is true . . . unless you are a pack rat.

The Collector's World

What any serious commitment needs most is wisdom, the insights that keeps the train of feelings from going off the rails of common sense. Collecting is no exception. Wisdom is the product of time, experience, and careful, objective study. What follows is a map for navigating the collector's world; I hope it qualifies as collectors' wisdom.

- ≈ Anticipation is the luscious and often overlooked part of collecting.
- ≈ Worries are limitless. So is enjoyment.
- ≈ Collecting may be a hobby, but it is more than that. It requires testing the depths that are inside us.
- ≈ Disappointment is inevitable. Learning from it is optional.
- ≈ Hope is the smile we see on the faces of successful collectors.
- ≈ Nostalgia may blind collectors to the current world of American antiques.
- ≈ The heart needs to attach itself to something outside itself or it withers.
- ≈ Our minds live in an unending past. Nothing disappears completely. All dwells in aura.
- ≈ Ironically and importantly, to collect successfully, you must trust others just as you yourself must be trustworthy.
- ≈ Antique hues speak of the past and the delights they brought.
- ≈ Each collector must decide the meaning of a piece's condition when considering and purchasing items for his collection.
- ≈ Dealers need to understand, where the eye leads, the heart follows.
- ≈ Ethics and rules of conduct exist for all residents in a community, including the village of American antiques.
- ≈ American antiques make history come alive and educate on the nation's present and future.
- ≈ As a wise man once said, "What we leave of ourselves becomes our selves." Our treasures have a life of their own.

- ≈ Fresh-to-the-market is more of a magical charm than a criterion.
- ≈ It is useful to consider what owning antiques truly entails and means.
- ≈ Collecting has proved to be, denied its atmosphere, a world denied, remembered, and yearned for.
- ≈ In collecting, objects might not be as valuable as what they make us feel.
- ≈ Collectors must resign themselves to confronting abundance without sacrificing delight.
- ≈ "Top Sellers" are a magnet for our attention. Enjoy but beware.
- ≈ Collectors need to learn about and master buying at auctions.
- ≈ Collectors decide how and what they choose to collect.
- ≈ Knowing about the various ways others try to influence collectors' purchases is critical to the hobby.
- ≈ Collectors spend a lifetime being prepared. They can never be too attuned to the market, have too much knowledge, or have too good an eye.
- ≈ Some collectors' pieces lie in plain sight, for others they are put away. What we love to collect determines this.
- ≈ Collectors purchase with high spirits and haunting ones.
- ≈ In timed auctions, often he who hesitates is saved.
- ≈ No matter what you collect, a collector must master style and connoisseurship criteria.
- ≈ Collectors need to hone their patience.
- ≈ The American antique community is vibrant and ever changing. There are stories waiting to be told.
- ≈ The true financial state of the American antique market would interest many.
- ≈ As noted, the antique dealer is often the bridge between things and enlightenment.

The Collector's World

Section I

A Plethora of Feelings:
What Collectors Experience and Why

Chapter 1

Anticipation

"'Well,' said Pooh, 'what I like best,' and then he had to stop and think. Because although Eating Honey was a very good thing to do, there was a moment just before you began to eat it which was better than when you were, but he didn't know what it was called."

A. A. Milne

Collectors spend a lot of time looking forward to, and unlike Pooh know what it is called – anticipation – the next show, an upcoming auction, a visit to a dealer's shop, or the next issue of a trade publication. Will the antique be as wonderful in person as it looks in photos and is described? Will I win the painting I have sought for years at the auction? Will I find something, anything, to fall in love with? Will it be affordable? Will a dealer have something pictured in an ad that I must follow up on immediately? There are a thousand and one ways we anticipate. But what exactly is anticipation and why is it an integral part of the collector's experience?

Anticipation is a state of expectation, of hope. More so, it is an excitement about the future and what may be. When we anticipate we eagerly await. We can be nervous when we anticipate but it is a good form of anxiety. What we anticipate is typically a positive outcome: The painting will be mine. While technically anticipation can be a state of biding one's time for a negative future event, we usually call such circumstances dread or apprehension – the proverbial trip to the principal's office at school or a dressing down at home we know is coming. In other words, anticipation is an optimistic feeling in the present about a future event, embodying the thought of what's next instead of (to some the more negative) what if? It is a way of speculating about the future, keeping a not yet occurring event fresh, playing it over in our minds and feelings.

∼

Thanks to Winnie the Pooh for as cogent a description of anticipation as we will find. By the way, a first edition (1926) of *Winnie the Pooh* goes for about $10,000. If you are searching for one, that is truly worthy of anticipation. Of course, anticipation is experienced differently by different collectors. For some, emotions tamped down in life and their personality, it may be more intellectual. For others, myself included, it is highly emotional, a yearning and wondering, adrenaline flowing as the auction nears the item I so dearly want to own, as the show doors open. For some, anticipation and what it brings allows the collector to maintain a fervor for assembling a collection, the disappointment of finding a piece one loves but already sold or with a price too high put in perspective, a part of "The Hunt" but not a calamity.

Anticipation is unavoidable. Our brain (even when we sleep) is constantly working and wondering about the future is part of that toil. Doing so gives shape and substance to the unknown and gives us energy. I think back to the intense anticipation of summer vacation when I was in elementary or high school. I could not wait for the softball games, sense of freedom, and hanging out. Anticipation, therefore, puts a positive perspective on future events and allows us to move forward to the future with some confidence.

Experience contributes to who we are, and influences anticipation. We draw from past experiences to fill in the future. Since we are more

Anticipation

comfortable with the positive, we will remember times when we found great objects at a show or auction. Those occasional "wins" as collectors sustain us, maintaining our anticipation. Collectors compare past experiences with future events, and these comparisons drive us to attend some shows (Have had good luck there, great pieces).

But we also keep track of striking out and avoid other venues (Have never found anything). Such disappointments are useful and should be a teaching moment for us. Did I misread the market and the cost of what I wanted at auction? In the future, do I need to look more carefully at the dealers listed for a show, so the antiques displayed there are more in line with what I collect? Depending on what a show specializes in and the price points of dealers, it is easy to understand why some collectors might anticipate them with relish, while others avoid them completely. Was my anticipation well placed? If I lost out to a higher bidder at auction, the disappointment I feel should not dissuade me from looking forward to the next opportunity. Such disappointment allows collectors to be open to a world that favors us only some of the time.

Of course, if you are a "glass is half empty" or the "glass is cracked" type of person, doom and gloom may be what you expect in the future. But sharing those "down" feelings tends to drive others away. Who wants to spend time with such a person? But if you anticipate a positive future, you are likely to be more upbeat, fulfilled, or happy. Thus, another purpose of such anticipation is to draw people to us, give us company and comfort, acquaintances or friends, people in our lives with whom to share our collecting fervor and spirit.

Part of anticipation, anticipatory thinking, allow us to imagine future events and to solve them in the present. We recognize and prepare for challenges before they occur. For example, collectors may think about how to move their pots of money around to afford an expensive piece they love and wish to purchase. Other collectors may do the same if they anticipate finding more than one antique at a show they cannot live without. Do I borrow from my credit union or pay it off over time? When we engage in anticipatory thinking, we are not trying to guess about the future but to note possible events that may pose problems. (As an aside,

A Plethora of Feelings

I would love to find two antiques, both pricey, I love, at the same show, and have to solve the problem of how to buy them both).

In essence, anticipatory thinking is the cognitive or non-emotional side of anticipation. We create various models of what may occur and the best ways we might proceed. Anticipation brings order and control to events that have not yet occurred. We are making pathways to goals (finding and owning antiques we love) before the auction begins or show door opens. Here also experience influences and improves our problem solving. Especially for a new collector, the thought of spending a year's antique budget on one object may be daunting. Experienced collectors who have done so before shrug their shoulders and soldier on.

Imagine collecting without anticipation. A collector goes to a show, finds nothing, and goes home. No anticipation. Something would be missing, in my mind a key part of the collecting experience, something to bask or luxuriate in. Oh, how I looked forward to spending some money and adding to my collection. Researchers talk about the joy of anticipation. Even if we find nothing to purchase, the anticipation in and of itself enriches our lives. Some research argues that anticipation is more intense than nostalgia, i.e., our feelings about future events are more intense than what we feel when looking back.

I attend Antiques Week in Manchester, New Hampshire each year. There have been years when I returned home with nothing. Yet the trip was still a grand success. I looked forward to landing in Manchester, getting in my rental car, and knowing I was there, shops to visit, good seafood of which to partake. I even looked forward to the drive home, typically late at night after arriving back in Milwaukee. Whether I had purchased any antiques or not I would be satisfied and already looking forward to next year.

One element of collecting antiques I believe some dealers miss or do not give enough weight to is that a great deal of the satisfaction and meaning for collectors does not derive from antiques themselves. When attending shows in Manchester I reunite with antique collecting friends I see there only annually, with good conversation waiting in line for the shows to begin. I say hello to dealers I like and see each year, wishing them a good show, being part of Antiques Week. The experience of connecting with people cannot be overstated as important and an integral part of collecting. In other words, I, like many other collectors, look forward to others' company and derive satisfaction from the world of collecting and those who inhabit it, equal to and sometimes more (egad!) to the stuff I dearly love to pursue and want to call my own.

As you might expect, anticipation may decrease when we are distressed. When troubled or worried we focus on the here and now, trying to remove or minimize the stressors or roll with them. In such circumstances it may be difficult to direct our attention to future events. Therefore, for some collectors, collecting takes a back seat in times of life or situational distress.

But not for all collectors. Since collecting is a hobby, I hesitate to say ancillary to central life events, anticipation may help collectors get through tough times. It can be a haven in a world full of pain, something pleasurable in a world of loss. Existentially all we have is the present, but if that present is painful, looking forward (anticipation also takes place in the present) to a positive future can be powerful. Collector anticipation can be a refuge, and keep us moving, put things in perspective, motivate us, for example, to be around people again.

Some writers about anticipation consider it one of the core feelings in the world, Pooh is a wonderful example. Waiting can be a thrill regardless of the outcome. Is nothing better than anticipating Christmas morning as a child? A collector of American antiques might respond, "Yes, the feeling of waiting for a prestigious show to open with wonderful pieces on the show floor." Anticipation also keeps us motivated and captivated, between shows or auctions when our collecting lives may slow down. There will be another show, dealer's shop visit, or auction in the future and, of course, we hope to find a piece of our dreams.

Truth be told, anticipation is also created within us by others. I think of auto dealers in the 1950s who put butcher paper over their showroom windows so we could not see what the new models looked like until their unveiling. Now in the antique world an auction house displays a few photos of pieces in an upcoming auction, then more photos, then a brochure, and finally a catalog. Dealers have taken to showing thumbnail photos of pieces they will be revealing in full and for sale at some future date, in essence a teaser creating intrigue. Scheduled website updates are gaining in popularity and serve the same purpose. All these marketing stratagems are aimed at increasing collectors' anticipation and our wanting. Feelings of celebration also create anticipation as shows invite us back to familiar surroundings for a "great" experience.

A well-known saying states: "Revenge is a dessert best served cold." The idea is well exemplified in Alexandre Dumas' *The Count of Monte Cristo* (1844) when Edmond Dantès, falsely accused and imprisoned, escapes. Guided to a fortune in treasure he reappears as the mysterious *Count of Monte Cristo* to avenge himself on those who conspired to destroy him. It is the anticipation of how he will go about seeking his redemption and wondering how the villains will get their comeuppance that provides the novel's tension. Such anticipation is luscious.

While our anticipation as collectors may not be as delicious or dramatic as Dantès' I hope that we at least enjoy it as much as Pooh did. For on occasion the honey follows and flows. Whether furniture or textile, painting or small, may the honey be yours.

Anticipation is the luscious and often overlooked part of collecting.

Chapter 2

A Collector's Concerns

Ours is a typical collection of Americana, a bit of this and a bit of that. Once set down in our home, pieces tend to stay put, gather some dust and become familiar friends. We enjoy their ambiance, their soft patina and advanced age, and do not think about them except when they call our attention. Oh, occasionally, when packing up a room's worth of smalls when the painter comes or moving furniture so the oriental rugs under them can be cleaned, we are reminded of more quiet, disquieting questions. How much of what we own is not right? How many times were we deceived or taken, deliberately or not? How hard did we fight to find and purchase them? How might we make a different choice now?

Every collector has those moments of insight into himself and the items he has. He asks himself, If I knew then what went on in the American antique business, how would I feel? Would I shudder, soldier on, or do an about face and head the other way at double pace speed? Who can I really trust in my world of collecting?

This time, it was a quiet day, nothing on the calendar. I could drift slowly from task to task, pick out how I want to spend my time, just sit and think. For some reason my brain was stirred by doubts about our collection. I was trapped in one of those muses that strike us all, slightly separated from humdrum, not quite visionary. Then I heard a knock at the

A Plethora of Feelings

front door, not a raven tapping, no gentle rapping (Edgar Allen Poe would have been disappointed). A gent of indeterminate age – kind looking, soft around the edges, erect in posture, casually dressed – asked if he could enter, and for some incomprehensible reason I nodded. In he came.

We sat companionably across from one another in the living room. He looked around him, at the oriental rugs, the 18th century furniture, the clocks and redware and candle boxes and painted tin and candlesticks and coin silver. "Having some doubts?" he asked.

"Yes," I replied, "It would be good to know what around us is a marvel and what is junk, although I am fearful of what I might discover."

"Are you sure you want to know?" he said.

"What the hell," I muttered. "Oh, sorry for the swearword." I thought he had winced just a bit.

He rose. "Pick out a piece and let's see what you learn."

I pointed to a tavern table. A nice one, I thought. Second coat of paint, I had been told by the dealer from whom I purchased it, early second coat. Apron scalloped on all four sides with small, delicate Queen Anne feet. "Do you want the good news or the bad?" the man asked.

I did not know which to choose. I had given the table a close inspection before saying that I would take it. I didn't know if I had the courage or energy for bad news, so I said, "Good news first, if you please."

He didn't move closer to the table, didn't turn it over, didn't put it in better light. He simply said, "Scalloping is original, feet are right, good proportions, top is original to the base."

That left the paint, I said to myself, and then said aloud, "The paint?"

"Second coat," he said, "but early 1900s, only 120 years old, not as represented to you."

I could live with that, yet his statement was disheartening. One of my major worries as a collector is being taken, deceived, deliberately lied to. If a dealer had not looked at a piece closely enough, and oftentimes they do not, I could live with that, an honest error. But to be snookered was beyond the pale. I looked at the man. There was a blurriness to his contours, almost as if a soft light shone behind him.

"The dealer lied to me," I snapped.

"Yes," he responded. "The dealer knew the paint's age."

Well, that was that.

"Pick another object," he said. We had moved upstairs by then, but I do not remember doing so.

"The highboy," I said. "Is it what it is supposed to be, and perhaps equally important did I overpay for it?" Another concern I have as a collector is failing to know the marketplace, paying too much when I should have walked away or bargained more. Again, he didn't give the highboy a second glance.

"Good news or bad?" he said.

Here we go again, I thought to myself. I took a deep breath. "Let's change the dance; bad news first."

"Well, one of the finials is replaced, and yes, you overpaid but not by a lot."

"The good news?" I asked.

"Not a marriage, pretty much as represented. And before you ask, the dealer did not know about the finial, and he was correct that the replacement brasses also are 18th century. And the surface is true, original."

Whew! I thought. Nice to know.

We repeated the exercise several more times and a pattern emerged. Pieces purchased from one dealer with whom I had stopped doing business long ago seemed to have the most problems. Again, I could endure the niggling faults. I had had misgivings, talked with other collectors and a dealer or two willing to give me honest feedback, and made the decision to get a divorce from that antiquarian. My only regret was that I waited longer than I might have. "Part of the learning process," I whispered to myself.

"You are well advised to be skeptical," the man said, "but not cynical. The overwhelming majority of dealers are honest, trying to make a living. Mistakes can be made. I'd guess on average you have escaped from the worst of them."

I stood there, bemused. Buying antiques is, it would seem, more of a gamble than most of us suspect. Simply wading into the pool is risky, unless you have tested the depth. "This is your chance," he said, smiling. "What's next?"

I took a deep breath. I knew in my heart what was next. I had tested him with pieces I was convinced had a reasonably sound provenance. It was time to move to the easily faked pieces in our collection. "Weathervanes," I said. We own several purchased from several different dealers – a couple of horses, a gamecock or two. To my disappointment we had never found a horse pulling a sleigh, one we could afford.

"Good news or bad?" the man said.

Dang, but how could that umbra follow him around, even in the dark corners? I needed a break. "Cup of coffee?" I asked.

"Sure," he said.

Boiling the water, pouring it into the French press, and preparing the teapot for my own brew gave me a bit of time to collect myself. Sipping my tea calmed me. "Okay," I said. "No good news or bad, give it all to me at once." And he did. One weathervane in average condition having a horse pulling a sulky – our worst weathervane to my way of thinking – was original. "Of course," I said to myself. A Jewell horse had had the tail replaced, but long ago. A painted gamecock was an outright fake. The other gamecock with a wonderful surface was fine. Ethan Allen had a wonderful surface and was all original. An eagle also was fine.

"And you conclude?" he said to me.

"Not bad," I said. "I beat the law of averages."

He smiled sadly and nodded.

"I cannot afford to be one of those purists who only purchase vanes pictured *in situ* in old photographs. I try to buy from dealers with respected reputations."

The man looked at me. "Vanes are tricky," he said. "You have to trust the dealer. Even experienced sellers get baffled by some of the stuff on the market. No surprise the average buyer gets led down the garden path now and then."

Ah, I thought to myself, a fourth collector concern. Besides outright trickery, dealers or auction houses making honest mistakes in their descriptions and my overpaying there is the issue of who a collector can trust. "Any advice how to tell who is trustworthy?"

He paused, took a sip of coffee. "Probably nothing more I can add that you do not already know. Talk with other collectors, get to know a

A Collector's Concerns

variety of dealers, develop you eye, the usual. But you will never bat a thousand," he concluded.

If anything niggles at the conscience of collectors it is their own mistakes, made in the past or waiting to be made. All collectors know they are eventually going to make them. The hard part is facing up to them.

I told what I had come to think of as my guardian angel exactly that and he came back with, "What's your baseline?"

"What do you mean?" I said.

He smiled at me. I thought fondly, How many mistakes do you allow yourself to make out of every ten items purchased? How the dickens does one reply to a query like that?

I fumbled, tried to be truthful and modest at the same time. "If I am buying something I think of as central to our collection, an item my wife and I really want, I spend a lot more time on . . . homework, research, bargaining, I hope I fail no more than ten percent of the time. For smalls, painted boxes, for example, 50% would be tolerable. They are more for the look than anything else."

That earned me a pat on the arm. "When you are chasing that highboy or tavern table, work with the best of dealers. But – what's that old line? 'Trust but verify.' I always tell folks that the outcome is only as good as the input. Spend time, think, consult. Collections are not the result of impulse but of the use of your intelligence, experience, and feelings."

"As for your painted boxes . . ." he added. "Do I really want to know?" I grumped. "Well, you don't have zillions of them, and you did okay." How he concluded that without inspecting them or even getting up from his chair was beyond me. But I believed him. He was most persuasive.

"What other concerns do you have?" he asked.

"The malarkey phenomenon," I replied. It was the first time he looked nonplused.

"Not in my dictionary," he said. "Can you elaborate?"

"Sure," I said. "Dealers extol the virtues of what they have in stock, as well they should. They are salesmen. Collectors know this. But occasionally we are convinced of the merits of a piece when perhaps – how should I say this? – we should have chewed before swallowing the baloney."

"Oh." A sip of coffee. (How could it stay hot for so long?) "By malarkey you mean being sold the piece rather than it talking to you."

Whoever he was, I thought to myself, he certainly knows about collecting for the issue of inanimate objects talking to collectors was true, verified, replicated but not well known outside the various collecting communities.

"Young man, I like that turn of a phrase. Can I borrow it in the future?" I felt flattered and agreed enthusiastically. He changed his focus, glanced to his left, and offered another insight, somehow intuiting the struggle my wife and I had gone through when we made the decision to write a rather substantial check. "Your first drop front desk," he said. "Great proportions as described to you, repairs honestly stated, a fan in the document door. But the fan isn't the best, and it has been refinished, albeit some time ago. When you purchased it, original finish was not as important to you as it is now, and you had not yet decided you were an 'original finish man.'"

(How did he know that?) I liked the sound of that, an "original finish man," almost like the Marlboro Man, rugged individualistic.

"Another piece?" he asked.

I had one in mind. "The triple back Windsor chair in the den," I said. We hadn't been in the den, but I knew that would make no difference for him.

"Which one?" he asked. "The rocker or the other one?"

"The other one," I said.

"Absolutely as described to you, great cant to the back, second coat of paint, a nice worn green, no replacements or repairs."

"The malarkey?" I asked.

"You never did ask the dealer how old that second coat of paint, the green is," he answered.

"Newer than I wanted," I said. "I fell in love with the chair and his words and lost sight of the bigger picture."

"Yup," was all he said.

"Another question . . ." I began.

"You know," he interrupted, "almost everything in life can be spoiled by insisting on total understanding. Do you know why the Mona Lisa is smiling?"

I glanced at him, and somehow, I was sure he knew the answer to that. He didn't say, though. I was glad.

"Well then, one last question," I insisted.

"Go ahead."

I did, the question any collector would ask, "Is there anything I have here that simply is not what I think it is?"

"You mean like the redware pitcher on the kitchen shelves."

"Oh, I know that is French," I said.

"How about the small ice cream table and four chairs in the front porch?"

"Not that old," I said."

"Then, no," he said, "nothing I can find."

Like any collector, the list of itchy concerns was endless. If something happened to my antiques, would my insurance company come through as promised? What to do with my collection when I was past loving it was a serious concern (see Chapter 15). And with dealers and experts aging (just as I was), I worried knowledge and research of locales, genres, and craftsmen might fade into history. I worried about my caretaking. I had recently found a wool blanket sitting in a basket neither my wife nor I had attended to in years, a moth hole attesting to our neglect.

He carefully put the cup on the table and stood, a bit shakily I thought. He touched my hand, and I felt a current passing between us. "By the way, I never got your name." It just hung in midair.

"Not important," he said. "Glad to be of help."

I awoke from my unintended nap with a start. For some reason, I was happy. I looked at the pieces around me and realized that the one thing I never even considered was a time when my Americana would no longer bring me delight.

Worries are limitless. So is enjoyment.

Chapter 3

Courage

The great – from Homer to George Washington to Winston Churchill – have long been fascinated by courage. And who can blame them? Bravery on the field of battle is one of the most admirable and inexplicable virtues imaginable. Then how and why can we indulge ourselves, talking about "bravery" in the pedestrian field of antique collecting?

The answer strikes me as persuasive, if not obvious. Examinations of courage provide us with object lessons: We learn to be better by assessing, evaluating, and imitating the behaviors of those who have acted admirably. Those actions do not have to be confined to the world of armed conflict or the world of political struggles (see Abraham Lincoln if you need an example) or even medicine (Madame Curie). Our varied worlds, including antique collecting, offer examples of individuals acting wisely, selflessly, and contrary to popular opinion.

Courage is defined as facing, usually with equanimity, something that is frightening. Courage involves doing the opposite of what common sense would tell us. Running toward danger rather than fleeing, risking personal wealth to preserve something most people would abandon, even enduring criticism rather than conforming to popular opinion, and we shall see these and other traits in action as we progress in our deliberation. Courage can be psychological as well as physical - strength in the face of pain, grief, or difficult uncertainty. It can be marked by action.

Courage

I differentiate between risk takers and those with courage. Risk takers may not know the consequences of their actions but have decided their hoped-for outcome is worth possible negative consequences. Those with courage may be risk-takers but they feel compelled to move forward because of a belief, a moral code or imperative. Those who behave courageously may believe in a better future for others (the downtrodden, posterity), some evanescent philosophy, their faith, family, their antique collection, the future, and survival of American antiques.

Anyone who collects antiques knows about passion, about following one's heart even when one cannot articulate the reasons for purchasing a specific piece. We collect what we do because we appreciate and love the genre. We want to build a collection. Collectors know of the competition in the auction house or in a dealer's booth at a crowded show, know that to develop a truly satisfying collection that reflects one's interests and uniqueness, a collection different from others, may mean taking chances. The "courage of one's convictions" is most relevant for collectors and dealers. When we act because of what we believe, sometimes courting failure or firmly facing the disapproval, even ostracism, of people we respect.

There is also "fool's courage," under which people do brave things trusting that some mysterious, kindly force will protect them. While some collectors may dream of an antique collector's god or goddess who offers such protection, I have never found one.

I assume it takes some courage to put a collection up for auction with your name prominently attached for the entire (antique) world to critique. Will the market value and respect the choices you made in what was purchased? To what extent does our reputation suffer if people think the collection is mediocre? What image of ourselves is being sent out for admiration, ridicule, or disdain? And if you are a private citizen – as opposed to a public figure – will anyone care? (They certainly will).

Israel Sack believed so strongly in this country and its traditions that he created a market in American antique furniture. In developing his business and sticking with it, he put his family's well-being and fortune at risk. He showed the courage of his convictions. So did Abby Aldrich Rockefeller who bought that "stuff" – folk art – because she liked it, long before it was recognized, researched, and required in any collection of Americana. While her collecting had little financial downside for someone of her wealth, in the face of ridicule she trusted her tastes. History proved her correct. Had history not validated her decisions, her name – if mentioned at all – might be greeted by curled lips. After all, there have been collections of art and jewelry in the past that were brushed off as "mere bagatelles." If Abby's folk art was dismissed as no better than the stuff we see on *American Pickers*, wouldn't the adjective assigned to her pursuit have been foolish rather than gutsy? She collected (as Sinatra might have sung) "her way." To heck with conventional wisdom or the rules of the day. Rockefeller made the rules, as it turned out.

Abby was not the only collector in the forefront. Those who purchased paintings by Picasso, Monet, and numerous other artists – even Grandma Moses – when the artists were still alive and painting, showed the courage of their tastes when the cognoscenti were casually dismissing the works. People collected weathervanes before they were thought of as sculpture and became central (to many) in any collection of Americana. Outsider art has gained influence because of actions on the part of nervy collectors who appreciated it early on and stood up for the genre's legitimacy and desirability.

My point is this: If someone goes against prevailing opinion and risks precious resources and public disapproval because he believes in the aesthetic, historic or intrinsic worth of a genre or object, that takes guts. That's exactly what bravery is all about. Collectors and dealers who take the path less traveled, who persevere in the face of adversity, display courage. So do those who sacrifice great chunks of their resources to knowingly amass pieces everyone, at least in the moment, dismisses as unoriginal, aesthetically trite, and more *outré* than worthy. Of course, there is a chance the collector is merely delusional, a sucker, lacking in taste. Then again, "delusions" must stand the test of time and taste, and it is surprising how often what looks to be esthetically marvelous and classy ultimately proves to be little more than a popular *tchotchke* – 45 rpm records and Beanie Babies come to mind. And "taste" is such a variable. It does not just exist. It is made, the ones

Courage

who make it are those with courage and a willingness to put themselves behind what they personally value.

Well, I am no Rockefeller but I believe that I and many other collectors make our courage known by what we purchase, group together, and display. We also do it our way. My collection of American antiques has its idiosyncrasies. Displaying a Bachelder Battle of Gettysburg with pieces a hundred years older may to some tastes be jarring. I like it. To mix my wife's aviation posters with painted rope beds and blanket chests may be unique but it seems to work. To believe in wooden works clocks enough to own four of them (perhaps an act more of stupidity than courage) certainly reflects bravery (they are oh-so-difficult to keep running and can be a pain to coddle and endure).

In that vein, I applaud those who once opposed the habit of stripping the paint from furniture, who loved and preserved painted pieces and extolled their virtue. Thanks to them, I and other collectors can own painted pieces today. Those who saw and loved the ingenuity and just plain funkiness of make-dos or fragments, may have in their own way also been courageous.

The courage of one's conviction also comes to mind when collector buys a piece that has lingered on the market. After all, hasn't everyone else passed on it, found it wanting? Isn't fresh for sale more desirable? And what do we say about a collector who finds herself surprised to fall in love with a piece from a genre she has never explored, her first Hudson Valley painting for example? It takes courage to trust one's gut, one's emotional response, one's love for a piece.

Some collector courage is largely unnoticed. She who stretches financially to own an antique she loves may have a lump in her throat, a funny feeling in her gut, and a hole in her pocketbook, but she is willing to face (down) those feelings in the face of the lack of a safety net for her decisions. Despite her expectations, her ardor for Americana may not last and no guarantee exists that she will truly love, over time, the piece she is trusting her instincts to purchase. But she carries on. My wife and I experienced all of this when we purchased our first expensive antique.

Dealers also display the courage of their convictions. I imagine even becoming a dealer takes a certain amount of bravery, a faith in his tastes, confidence that there are others who will respect his expertise. In that case, the conviction is not generally in the thing (art dealers being an exception, I suppose) but in the process. What you see in their booths and shops are items they bought that they believe buyers will approve of, covet, and cherish. Knowing there may only be a few customers for a certain hooked or shirred rug, painted piece of furniture or an initialed redware plate, they still plow ahead. Of course, purchasers may not always validate their sense of antique worthiness and they may end up holding a piece for a long time or sell it at a loss. But they'll buy again and again. No longer do we live in those halcyon days before the Great Recession, when just about anything seemed to sell, often at, compared to now, high prices indeed. The so-called Good Times (for dealers) have not returned, instead exposing a collecting era when people move more carefully, and some spend less liberally. Dealers seem to work harder now, their courage more necessary.

There exists yet another form of dealer courage that might be explored: when one spends a great deal of money on an antique for stock, not representing a collector. For instance, a Hicks' Peaceable Kingdom was purchased for stock at over $1.5 million, and so was an Amni Phillips (gorgeous and I wish I could buy it) painting of a girl in a red dress for nearly the same amount. You must respect anyone willing to put his love of antiques and belief in a piece's inherent worth into a purchase of that magnitude. Here, the individual's faith is not in the painting but in his taste and expertise. Dealers need to believe in themselves more than in what they sell, I expect.

Another form of courage entails standing up for what is right. I remember a dealer who recognized that an item up for sale at a well-known auction house was a fake and used social media to spread the word. Some dealers and collectors rolled their eyes I am sure – believing that "buyer beware" is the cardinal commandment of the marketplace. Fortunately, the item was eventually removed from the auction. To act alone – as this dealer did – shows the courage to do what is right.

All dealers and collectors at one time or another face defeat or are haunted by memories of pieces that they should have purchased. In other words, collecting or selling both involve suffering. To bear it with dignity, faith in the future, or a spirit of respectful concession to the winner is classy. Dealers have suffered a lot in the last twelve years. So have some collectors. Those who stay involved, maintain their passions, and promote the health of the profession/hobby/ vocation are the folks we want to be around, to be like.

The sheer rarity of the bravery required to admit a collecting error should not be minimized, by the way. Human nature is not efficiently designed to admit personal blunder (a fact we are reminded of daily by listening to political leaders trying to explain why the perfect world they have promised in running for election has failed to materialize). It takes courage to admit I should not have bought a piece that I did, to admit an attribution to location or craftsman was in error, to state publicly I behaved inappropriately interacting with a dealer or at auction. Such honesty is both rare and welcome in our small universe of American antiques. I remember telling a dealer long ago, with trepidation, that I should not have purchased a piece I did from her. Much to my amazement she agreed, pointing out it did not fit in my collection, and she was surprised (but pleased) to hear me realize the error. My disclosure showed her I was growing as a collector and developing a higher level of style and connoisseurship. Sometimes courage has its rewards.

While waiting in line for an antique show to open and talking with other collectors I have reluctantly (at least the first few times I did so) admitted to collecting mistakes fearing reprobation or a snarky response. To my surprise, I found that other collectors often wanted to hear more about my mistakes and even offered to share some of their own. I learned important collecting lessons by listening to other screw-ups and quite clearly so did the people who listened to me.

Collecting to many is more than a mere hobby, a passing fancy, or the redistribution of excess wealth. By examining courage in collecting, we better understand the complexities inherent in our world of American antiques. Churchill once said that "Success is not final. Failure is not fatal. It is the courage to continue that counts." Yes, we make mistakes as collectors. Yes, it takes time and nerve to build a solid collection. The process can be daunting and disheartening. What we say and spend our money on reflects our visions as collectors or dealers. Sometimes we must have the heart to march to our own drummer. Now and then we must overcome obstacles, act unselfishly, reach for the moral high ground, or fly in the face of conventional wisdom. It is hardly too much to call a response to challenges such as that "courage."

Collecting may be a hobby, but it is more than that. It required testing the depths that are inside us.

Chapter 4

Disappointment

Every collector, whether one who pursues Americana to another who lusts after classic cars, knows what disappointment is. Disappointment, after all, is inherent to collecting, always lurking. I have experienced disappointment time and again. For the moment it squelches my passion. No matter how frequent my successes, I am still let down about pieces I failed to acquire or overlooked. All of this got me thinking. What is it I am exactly feeling when I am disappointed and what is its place in collecting?

The circumstances that lead to disappointment are clear to me – or at least I think they are until a new set of them arises. For instance, I am dismayed when I find an antique that I truly love, but my wife does not. Taking her feelings into account I sadly pass. But a sadness, a sense of missed opportunity, a hint of personal frustration lingers.

Or take an example from an auction. I find a piece I believe has potential and obtain more detail on its condition. Being seriously interested, I attend an auction preview, look at the object, have its worth confirmed by someone more expert than I am. There I sit, charmed, anxious and hoping for a shot at owning such a treasure. When the item comes up for bid, I never get my paddle in the air. The object sells for far more than I can afford. My taste and connoisseurship have been confirmed, much to my dismay. The irony, readily apparent, is bittersweet. Other times I wait in line for several hours at an antique show. I enter once it opens and do a quick walk through. There it is: a piece I have been seeking for some time. My heart quickens and I can feel it doing so. As I approach the marvel, I notice the small red dot affixed to it. The treasure is sold. Someone beat me to it. Sometimes I drive to a dealer's shop. He has emailed he has a piece he believes I will truly love. The antique is exactly as he described it, but my heart sits still. It fails to speak to me.

All these scenarios that we collectors encounter lead to frustration, jealousy, and disappointment. Frustration can be handled by being persistent. Jealousy can be dealt with by anger, meditation, or good wine. Somehow, at least to me, the downcast feeling I get from being disappointed is different.

Disappointment lies on a continuum of severity. To propose to the woman of your dreams and have her say "No, the time is not right, I do not love you the way you do me" is a punch in the gut. You may mope for weeks, months or longer. Your world is sour, gray, sad, depressing, unfair. You are convinced this is an existential downer. No one else will ever come close to her. You will never love again. But if I see a toy airplane that I am contemplating purchasing for my wife's collection that upon inspection is not up to her standards, I may be mildly disappointed, but life goes on, immediately. There will be other, better pieces and I can mutter "next time" coldly and with little sense of loss.

Disappointment occurs when our hopes or aspirations are thwarted. Usually we feel sad, regretful, deflated, despondent, let down, or dissatisfied. Disappointment, the product of a "bad" outcome, acknowledges a loss. Something one has hoped or wished for has gone "a'glimmerin" as the Irish say. In the case of the toy airplane, something is not as good as I thought; the movie despite the glowing reviews was *meh*; the meal at the fabled restaurant only average.

Notice that high expectations greatly increase chances of disappointment. The more firmly you rest your hopes on something, set your heart's desire on someone, and that hope is unrequited, the more probable (and possibly more severe) the disappointment.

Disappointment, then, is the result of the strength of an anticipated outcome and the failure to find it on your part. Some people bounce back quickly from these nagging disasters, some do not. Optimists, in particular – the glass is half full or very full individuals – often struggle bitterly finding the glass not only empty but perhaps even absent. For some of them, disillusion is a rare event, mostly because they are inclined find almost everything hunky-dory. In contrast, I am a realist. I know the fat lady is perfectly capable of singing off-key, that not every potential purchase is as perfect as I hope, that no guardian angel will protect me from the invasive bidder who snatches the perfect piece out of my grasping fingers.

As all collectors know, we do not live in a perfect world and disappointment is one feeling that reminds us of the imperfect world we find ourselves in. We do not always get what we want and do not always get what we deserve (or think we do). The power wielded by sheer chance is unavoidable, despite our best efforts, even our deep-rooted faith in our abilities to win the prize we covet. Disappointment, paradoxically, makes it all the sweeter in the few cases where we fall in love with an antique and become its owner (caretaker). The inevitability of disappointments serves a purpose: It keeps us from being as thoroughly spoiled as we might be if everything went our way.

Surely every collector has seen an antique at a show or on a website that she would be delighted to live with, dallied and dithered and found it sold and herself disappointed when she returned to look at it again. The cliché, "He who hesitates is lost" is not entirely built on weary wisdom. But collectors also hear enough cries of, "Look before you leap" – and if you do not, you may be disappointed with the quality of what falls into your hands. The sneaky thing about folk wisdom is that it encapsulates experiences, not that it forecasts the inevitable. For every horse sold without the buyer examining its teeth, a Man O' War is out there being sold for a pittance. Some things are out of our control, luck does play a part in collecting, and disappointment is unavoidable but need not be chronic.

Nonetheless some collectors are disappointed individuals. No matter the quality of the outcome, the marvel of the antique they have spent time and money pursuing, what they end up with never quite meets their expectations. For them, every silver lining has a cloud. For these (fortunately) outliers, it is as if a psychological evil eye is looking down and ruining what should have been a wonderful and positive experience. Without their anomie, they would be someone else – maybe satisfied, perhaps cheerful, hopefully tolerable. They must talk about their deflated view of the world we live in and their sufferings, and they have oh-so-much to bear and share. After all, "The antique could have been even more perfect, the price even more fair, the story behind the piece even more interesting." You get the point.

All the above may be known to collectors. But there is more to disappointment than abstruse analysis or even smarmy comments about pessimists. Disappointment can be a source of very real psychological stress. And while some of us are either impervious or grow used to it, some of what we do and decide is still based our desire to avoid being disappointed. To understand disappointment more fully we need to turn to a field called "decision analysis."

In this instance, decision analysis (a very broad field, indeed) theorizes that people assess the probability of disappointment and make decisions that are likely to minimize it. It is part of human nature not to want to be disappointed. Let's look at examples from the world of collecting, a caricature to be sure, but useful, returning to the auction house, to see what this means. Sotheby's January Americana auction has a piece that on our hypothetical collector's computer screen looks wonderful. He has been seeking it for years. Yet he is hesitant to ask someone to look at it in person because he may learn that the item is flawed in ways he cannot discern from a distance. Even if the report comes back positive, he may be hesitant to travel to New York to look at the piece himself. After all, he cannot be the only person seeking such a wonderful antiques and others have more financial resources than he does. "Why bother to bid?" he asks himself. Only one outcome would be positive (the antique proves marvelous, affordable, and weakly contested) and there is such a host of potentially disappointing consequences. He could be outbid. Perhaps a well-known dealer with deep pockets is the winning bidder (this happened to me once, though I did not find it particularly off-putting). Realistically, this Croesus might not even be interested in the piece. If the collector were me, instead of this pussycat, I would tell myself, Go for it because occasionally the dice roll my way. But our avoiding collector may just sit in his study, feeling safe, and stew.

Disappointment, and this may surprise people, has positive purposes. Yes, it brings with it a feeling of sadness. And sadness helps us remember rather than wanting to forget. Sadness typically begets self-inspection. We feel, sometimes intensely, the loss of something or someone we wanted in our life and try to make sense of that loss. Thus disappointment (sadness) can influence future behavior in positive ways. We may not let the love of our life get away so easily the next time. As for collectors, disappointments that are a product of their own behavior may drive them to trust their judgments more, to travel to New York for that Sotheby auction, or to develop greater acceptance of the vicissitudes of their (collecting) lives.

Disappointment also may point us in better directions. A collector may learn not to covet objects he surely cannot afford. He may appreciate them, lust after them, wish himself as Tevye sings in *Fiddler on the Roof,* "If I was a rich man," but not be disappointed when those who truly can afford the piece end up with it. If we learn that we cannot own pieces that meet many of our style and connoisseurship criteria, we may narrow our focus to one or two items that mean the most to us – and be happy with our furniture collection with original finish even if the pieces' scales are not perfect, or be proud of our collection of boxes with ornamentation (but none too fancy because these are beyond our means), or enjoy our coin silver spoons, tongs and small ladles, even if they lack important attributions to the craftsman who made them.

Disappointment may point a collector to ask the most important questions in collecting: "Who am I as a collector?" "What do I love?" "What objects give my life meaning?" These "existential" questions of collecting arise time and time again in our lives, but the struggle in seeking their answers, I believe, brings depth, purpose, and wisdom to what we do. For the moment at least, the posing and answering of these questions create an opportunity to remember the mistakes we have made, reminisce over what we have and have not accomplished with fondness instead of pain, and as noted above, realign our collecting goals.

That is the paradox: Disappointment may be good for us. Because we are human, at times we will consciously or unconsciously realign our thinking and behaviors to avoid disappointment, and not necessarily to our benefit. The defense mechanism of rationalization is one such example. I see an antique I love. I want it! I cannot, for a variety of reasons, have it. And just like the fox leaping for the luscious grapes in Aesop's Fable I may decide, it was no good (the grapes were sour) anyway. The danger lies in the fact that doing so erases the benefits and lessons disappointment can teach us. And until we confront ourselves with the reality, "I cannot always have what I want" (sounds like a 5-year-old having a tantrum, doesn't it?) we will be stuck as discontented collectors, unhappy and filled with rue. It is easier to protest about our unjust universe than to see life as it really is, but not necessarily better.

Once again, I am struck by the complexity of the collecting world. What seems so evident and simple is seldom so. Collectors who overvalue happiness and serenity may benefit less compared with those who acknowledge disappointment as an inevitable part of living a full life, and certainly with a collecting one. I agree with Henry David Thoreau, "If we will be quiet and ready enough, we shall find compensation in every disappointment." That compensation may involve a deeper self-understanding and, in our world, even access to some very fulfilling – albeit imperfect – treasures.

Disappointment is inevitable. Learning from it is optional.

Chapter 5

Hope

"Hope is the thing with feathers that perches in the soul – and sings the tunes without the words – and never stops at all."
Emily Dickinson

"To live without hope is to cease to live."
Dostoevsky

Most collectors know (and I have written about it myself, see *Come Collect with Me*) that one of the primary motivators for collectors is The Hunt. Not knowing when one will find a piece to covet, even what it will be, renders the ongoing search full of unknowns. The Hunt lies at the heart of what we collectors do and is therefore important.

Recently, I was reminded of the central role played by The Hunt when I reread Jeanne Schinto's wonderful five-part *Maine Antique Digest* series about The Walpole Society, that group of men (only men always) whose donated collections filled museums, Americana wings and exhibits. Their discoveries began in the latter 19th century and gifts early in the 20th century and beyond, though dwindling as time passed. The problem is, of course, is that true treasures are extremely difficult to find nowadays.

A Plethora of Feelings

The character of the quest for the exceptional has also changed. Now pickers may go door to door in rural areas, rooting out valuables ... along with the plethora of junk. Instead of holding on to pieces, owners market them on-line or send them off for auction. What has largely vanished are instances of moneyed men pulling Philadelphia fine furniture out of chicken coops for pennies on the dollar – The Hunt, however, even then, an endless chore. If one interviewed current Walpole Society members, I am willing to bet even they would speak of hope. Despite the difficulties stumbling across obscure, long-lost treasures they still have faith their searches will pay off.

Put simply, they like the rest of us have hope – the fuel of collectors, the currency that motivates and inspires much of what we must do. We keep looking for the attainable ideal, full of faith that the antique world's gods and goddesses are on our side or at least remain neutral, full of hope that we will prevail. Despite all these facts, I have seen nothing written about hope as it applies to collectors. My subsequent search and pondering unearthed more than I anticipated.

Hope, of course, is not the sole purview of collectors, and it is no small element in human existence, as even the classical writers acknowledge. Pandora's Box legendarily contained hope (the goddess *Elpis*) and there are several theories as to why hope remained in her box and was not loosed on the world. Since hope is seen as a power that comes to humans from the gods, it was their decision to keep this gift trapped. *Spes* in a more recent – if not by much – legend is the Roman equivalent of the Goddess *Elpis* and is revered as the divine personification of the cynosure of the Virtues. Biblically, hope is the belief that what God has promised will come true in time. Throughout our history hope has been called upon to sustain people in times of great travail, those moments sometimes called "the dark night of the soul" – times of war, famine, and disenchantment. The human desire for a better future is almost overwhelmingly powerful. The concept of hoping is visibly captured inside the American Dream, that my children's future will outshine my own.

Were it not for the fact that hope perches in our souls we might cease to live (and I add, might cease to collect). Its powerful influence is buoyant. It lifts the collector's mood and thoughts. It makes The Hunt tolerable, even exquisite. Instead of sinking under the disappointments of collecting, hope sustains us. While the future is unknowable, hope makes it, if one paints with a wide brush, at least less mysterious. It enables collectors to fill in some of the dark corners of the future. And what dissipates shadows is positive. "Things will work out. I will add to my collection if I keep at it."

Hope, in other words, is mightily attached to desire. The stronger the latter the more likely you are hopeful. Ambiguity is washed away, and the desire becomes truth. "I will find what I am looking for." As delusional as it is, the very presence of hope makes our lives better. Never knowing when and where a desired addition to my antique collection will be found, the presence of hope makes The Hunt bearable. Being buoyant and positive about the future makes it more likely my hopes will be. The collector continues to bid at auction, to attend shows, to keep in touch with dealers. Instead of becoming helpless in the face of a vague future, the hopeful collector works to make events bend to her advantage.

Collectors' actions show that hope is not simply mere pie-in-the-sky wishing but is built on a belief (a) that a future goal can be fully realized, (b) that multiple paths to that goal can be actively pursued, and (c) that they have the skills to find and own desirable treasures (not all the time, of course, but often enough).

A collector's hope is like an old friend offering encouragement. The always-lurking temptation despair is minimized or vanishes altogether in its presence. Despair is of course the opposite of hope, the feeling that the future never works as one wishes. All alternatives for action are negative. No matter what I do, the outcome will be distasteful at best, perhaps disastrous. Collectors may not be aware of the degree to which hope fuels their activities but without it they would be wed to unhappiness and eventually cease collecting.

We are fortunate that hoping does not have to focus on a single goal, and as we all know collectors carry with them a grab-bag of ambitions. I am resigned to never finding a Windsor bench in original paint in a size our dining room will accommodate, at a price my pocketbook can afford. Somewhere deep down a little voice still cries out now and then than it could happen, but that cry is small by now and I have shifted my collecting ambitions to other, more attainable pieces and genres. The possibility of reaching obtainable goals sustains my hope and collecting continues to be fun and meaningful. Because I have sustained my hopes I can think, feel, and act as an effective collector.

It is important to distinguish between mere wishing and hoping. Wishing is passive and inspires no behaviors that reach for a desired outcome. Hope in contrast does precisely the opposite. It inspires grasping and working. Sheer optimism has no force or drive behind it either. It motivates no plans or actions. Optimism as the cliché has it puts lipstick on a pig, the best face on a situation one can conjure without changing the underlying reality. In addition to its hale effects on the collector, hope negates cynicism. The cynical collector bemoans the fact only the "well-to-do" can build great collections, for example, even though his budget for antiques exceeds what most collectors can afford. Cynicism is a form of resignation to a world in which one cannot happily live. With hope we can stride in that world more confidently.

Can auction houses or dealers materially affect the situation of an individual collector? Of course, they can. If The Hunt has failed us, someone can still whisper, "This object is different from the one you sought but it is marvelous in its own way." Our choice is simple, We can purchase it or others of what may be a new genre for us, or we stay and continue our search, or even do both. In brief, dealers and auction houses can be collaborators, encouraging us to broaden our interests and exposing us to a greater depth of history and research.

Collectors, themselves, can change their collecting focus. If a spice chest in wonderful condition is too costly, we may simply ask ourselves, What else do or might I like? or What else might grace and advance my collection? My wife and I have found, for example, that upgrading our Oriental rug collection is a dangerous (increasingly expensive) pastime, albeit satisfying so a piece must be extra special just to be considered. Rather than reaching higher and higher in the Americana market and finding pieces unattainable because of their cost, we have turned our attention to other antiques, in my case redware and in hers, Black dolls. Collectors need to collect to sustain their hope.

Collectors who are hemmed in by period and genre should learn from Shakespeare's Hamlet who says, "There is nothing either good or bad but thinking makes it so." When we collect, when we are involved in The Hunt, we need to have and (if such a thing is possible) exercise hope. Of course, bad things – and bad deals – really do happen in life and in collecting, but typically the ones arising from The Hunt are not catastrophic unless we make them so. If every collector who missed out on an object that he really wanted quit collecting, there would be few of us left.

The wise collector knows how to weather storms of disappointment, frustration, and conflict. If she is truly wise, she cuddles hope and keeps right on moving forward. Oh, all of us now and then bemoan our collecting fate and wander in a funk for a while, but most of us have perspective. There is something delightful, fulfilling, and ideal out there, waiting for us to find and capture it. We make it so.

Collectors, dealers, auction houses – the very roots of collecting Americana – are hopeful sorts. And that sparkling optimism is often rewarded. I think of the vast trove of goods that continually enter the market with auction after auction offering marvelous pieces to covet. Some of these pieces will be above our budget, others will fall into the hands of a collector more fervent, still others will be on closer examination sham or shoddy. Not a one of them will not be worth The Hunt, because that is where the fun and discovery (both of objects and ourselves) are, both important components of what collecting Americana is all about.

We collectors have above all to know ourselves: what fulfills us, what touches our sense of history, what brings life to America's past. By doing so hopes are born and nourished.

Hope requires dreaming. I dream of owning a wonderful Hudson Valley painting with all the traits that make them so cherished – figures on the shoreline, multiple boats sails sparkling, activity, life, brilliance. A dealer I have purchased from before has one I can afford, but I do not love it (of course). One is up for auction soon, as I write this that my wife and I do love but probably cannot afford (of course). Do I fall on my sword? I do not. Since hope is more than merely dreaming, I will continue to look. The Hunt continues. And other genres beckon me as I await the miracle. All is not lost.

Hope aside for the moment, I know my experiences, talents, and skills have and will continue to build a collection I can be proud of. Grit and perseverance will help. Personal traits and character are powerful tools, and their use is hot in psychology right now, both as a corrective and a trap. But hope itself remains undervalued as both an agency and pathway. A collector filled with hope is determined to build a treasured collection and employs different strategies to reach that never-quite-finished goal. One of my strategies, tongue in cheek, is to drive a 40-foot moving van to Colonial Williamsburg or Historic Deerfield and simply empty the place out . . . as if it all would fit. Talk about dreaming. Realistically I just keep plugging away, undiscouraged by the occasional failure, undaunted by the passing disappointment.

In my experience, collectors talk more about their hopes than they realize. When waiting in line for a show to open, many conversations take place about how collectors go about finding pieces they want. They are discussing how to overcome obstacles and move closer to cherished goals (and pieces of Americana). Let us debunk once and for all the notion that hope is nothing more than a "feel-good" emotion. It is a motivational system. Hope leads to action and if you act long and skillfully enough you will be successful. Not always, mind you, but often enough to encourage . . . hope. Will I find that Hudson Valley painting I so cherish? I believe I will. Notice that hoping involves something more than choosing easy goals and grasping them. Hard hopes require work, but the results can be blindingly wonderful.

It is poetic and theological to think of hope as dwelling in one's soul. And in its own way it does. But hope also can be gritty. To reach what one hopes to reach can take time, failure, dead ends, humility, and self-doubt. Hope makes life interesting if we follow its path to the end. Good collecting days for you and yours. And be filled with hope.

Hope is the smile we see on the faces of successful collectors.

Chapter 6

Nostalgia

"Nostalgia is a seductive liar."
George Ball, American diplomat and banker

All collectors eventually engage in nostalgia (from the Greek for homesickness and álgos – "longing"). It is, to be specific, a typically moody longing for the past, sometimes for a time or place that lives in blissful memory. As a long-time collector of American antiques, I confess to waxing nostalgia from time to time, ignoring the fact that "the good old days" are probably now, and the past was not as wonderful as I remember it. Yet in the midst of winter when I sit before a roaring fire cuddling a glass of single malt scotch, I mourn days gone by. Or when talking with other collectors, "Do you remember when. . .?"

To be human is to be nostalgic. The impulse and the practice are inescapable. We have a need to fantasize that our earlier lives (and the lives of bygone people) must have embraced a clarity, a purity, a meaning that are missing from our present existence. Our hearts are drawn back to a time perhaps, when life was simpler, or at least we remember it as being so, when the world was better. Nostalgia then, somehow marries our present selves to our past ones.

In more than one movie, the elderly British men sat outside around

A Plethora of Feelings

a small pub or café table in the town square, drinking wine, eating good home-baked bread or luscious stew, smoking, and baring fond remembrances. The Hun feared their resolve and might at arms. They were respected. And look, now snot-nosed kids poke fun at them, shapely maidens tell them not to drink so much ale or smoke so much tobacco, they have lumbago. Back when, they courted and bedded, roistered, and sang, life had meaning.

The melding of homecoming and loss speaks to one important drive behind collecting. Some collectors of American antiques yearn for a past way of life, nostalgic for how people lived in the 18th or 19th centuries. If so, nostalgia insulates them from reality: how frequently young people died and how hard life truly was compared with now. But they capture the days of yore often in their period New England homes or new abodes that look centuries old. Pieces in their collection, just like a trip to Colonial Williamsburg or Historic Deerfield, also recall life back then and probably what they imagine their lives would have been like. Who doesn't smile when one "ties one on" at a Williamsburg tavern (that is ties a large napkin around one's neck to protect expensive clothing, the source of that now-bibulous metaphor)?

The problem is that Proust was correct. "Remembrance of things past is not necessarily the remembrance of things as they were." My theme is a simple one: Too much nostalgia hinders collectors. If we want to be satisfied by our passion, we must collect in the here and now. I would add, however, that we are fully licensed to endow what we collect with attributes of glowing rosiness, even imagining what it must have been like to possess this precious bauble back then. Nostalgia is legitimate entertainment but a poor assessment instrument. Time moves on and collectors had best move with it.

What are we collectors nostalgic about? Many things as it turns out. I draw from personal experience, and I have talked to enough fellow collectors to know I am not alone in these remembrances. And if I miss instances, I have confidence my readers – you – can fill in the gaps.

Nostalgia says, **Wonderful antiques were more common and widely available**. In my memory perfect tables, paintings, or pieces of redware (see how fallible nostalgia is, I didn't even collect redware back

Nostalgia

then?) were easily found at every show and dealer's shop. Of course, older collectors when I began collecting decades ago were saying the same thing. Stillinger's *Antiquers: The Men and Women who were Responsible for the Changing Taste in American Antiques* probably felt the same way after more than once finding a colleague, but also competitor, had beat them to the farmhouse in his horse and buggy for the gem that he thought awaited only him. (How lucky they were, to tell the truth, that if missing out on one great piece, many more comparable ones were available, thus their donations of magnificent collections to build museums' holdings.)

For instance, many collectors will tell you that in the 1950s there were great antiques for sale, more than now. But there was a lot of dross, too, just like today. More than one collector has recently attended a show at which several pieces vied for his attention, all wonderful, all worth taking home. Young collectors may well look back to the early 2020s, years from now and remember how freely available good antiques were, now being the good old days for them.

My window on the 1950s or 1960s comes from the black and white photographs of dealers' booths or advertisements I see in books and or in American antique publications. Some wonderful pieces appear, especially brown furniture. And yet, one must keep in mind what does not appear – genres that are most desirable today were not collected by many in the 50s or earlier. I especially think of original paint and surfaces on furniture.

If you were a trend setter back then, and truly trusted your eye and taste, some forms of folk art would have been more available and less costly than now. Stoneware, painted tin, and other examples also might have been a "dime a dozen," but that was because few aesthetes wanted them. As we all know desirability waxes and wanes. But how many collectors truly are ahead of the curve in collecting American antiques? Not many I suspect.

Antiques were cheaper than they are now is another nostalgic memory one recollects and often believes. Yes, pieces were less expensive, but to throw a monkey wrench into our nostalgia, their prices should be increased by the rate of inflation in the intervening years to determine what a piece really cost its buyer. And certainly, after the great recession of 2008-09, when the American antiques' market reset itself except for the best of the best, many genres and pieces now may be thought of as cheap, inflation be danged.

Nostalgia also causes us to forget that for most of us our disposable income was much less then than it is today, many needs existed for our dollars – raising children, college costs, mortgage payments. I still remember a robin's egg blue blanket chest my wife and I could not afford at the lofty price of $1,300.00 – this was the early 1980s, almost 40 years ago. That was a fortune to us. Antiques may not be more expensive now, but the resources of collectors may be greater and more suitable to the market.

Another nostalgic remembrance: **The past was replete with kinder and gentler people than collectors encounter today**. We remember the dealers we bought from as being more honest perhaps, more helpful. This legend is certainly idyllic for looking at our American antique community with blinders off and nostalgia safely tucked away, schnooks and crooks have always existed, fakes passed off as the real thing, undisclosed enhancements made to pieces. Then as now a certain cadre of dealers have earned the respect and trust of collectors, and a few have not.

Dealers were more epic then and had better inventory, or so we think. Oh really? There are dealers out there right now who are on the cusp of becoming legends, sometimes for their expertise, often for their honesty, now and then for their nose in sniffing out treasures.

Marrying the nostalgic belief that great antiques could be readily found years ago, that they were much cheaper than at present, and that a cadre of wonderfully gifted dealers had no higher ambition than serving buyers, some imagine **it was easier to build a collection back then than it is now**. I, for one, suspect such easy generalizations. Building a collection has always required perseverance, sound judgement, a good eye, solid relationships with dealers, courage, and a questioning character. Still, in our nostalgic moments we believe that if only we had lived 50 years ago, oh the collection we would have amassed!

Sometimes the past we yearn to inhabit really was better, or at least different. That undeniable fact, some venues were wonderful, feeds nostalgia. *The Winter Show* and antiques' month in New York City used to be the cynosure for American antiques. Some argue that Antiques Week in Manchester was better years ago. I admit to being one of them. The array of offerings then seemed superior to now. At least that is how I remember it and I will leave it to others to tell me if I am deluding myself. One dealer recounted he thought there was more buying and selling back then and almost all dealers had good shows, a belief supported by another who said that what he sold at one of the shows provided three months of profit for the business. Yet it doesn't matter, a collector must cope with the market today.

We also can be nostalgic for characters. I am told that there were more eccentric dealers, just as there used to be more eccentric faculty at the university where I taught. Eccentricity seems and is rarer nowadays. There was a time when characters took pride in being different and thought it created an image. The Tom Thumbs and Merlins of the collecting world became legends in their time and the source of stories still being passed about our little community.

When was the last time a dealer wore a cape and hat? Such expressions of individualism and affectation seem gone. How many dealers now kick you out of their shop if they don't like you or think you are not serious about their wonderful pieces. Roger Bacon was truly larger than life, a former Shakespearean actor who performed in the antique world, including a routine with his wife about a piece's asking price and what it cost them. A doyen in the antique world had the greatest breadth of any dealer then and now. Gruff, tough, and smart he could be unpleasant but had great taste to go with his fierce aggressiveness. The famous, respected woman dealer who looked like the little old lady in Tweety Bird cartoons held court in her booth as some other dealers did also. The dealer who brought no inventory to a show but stocked her booth with what she bought on the floor. The gay dealers of flamboyant personality, the first-generation Jewish dealers with Yiddish heard. Larger than life in so many ways indeed.

Nostalgia has its own oddities, like the dealer who mourns for the boom-and-bust cycle that used to be more common. He observed that even with the pandemic dealers showed great stability, with few going out of business. "Too stable," he said apparently believing ours a dull world.

A Plethora of Feelings

This same dealer missed the debauchery that used to be more common, as he remembers it. There certainly were more country New England house sales with goods that hadn't seen the light of day for generations. The rumored presence of undiscovered American antique treasures in barns and outbuildings provided many collectors with a delightful excuse to motor about the countryside and undying memories when something came to hand for a reasonable price. Those days are, unfortunately, almost completely gone.

I am told also that auctions used to be the realm of dealers competing with other dealers, because collectors wanted to know if the pieces that they purchased were "right." Another dealer told me the business has changed: more collectors want "the look, with fewer collectors exhibiting connoisseurship." Is he being nostalgic? Is it true that collectors were more discriminating, more concerned with authenticity, more *au courant* at an as-yet undiscovered era gone by than they are today?

Nostalgia is almost always a form of needed illusion, blinding us to the realities of collecting in the present. For example, I must constantly tell myself how difficult it is to judge an antique from photographs without being able to touch, hold, look, and really see it. Amidst those handicaps, some flowers still bloom. My wife and I recently purchased a child's chair I liked. When it arrived, it was ten times more beautiful and desirable than the photos led me to believe. I am sure I have missed out on pieces I would have wanted had I only seen them in person.

Another reality are the new shows and auction houses that have sprung up. To add successfully to my collection, I must become acquainted with them.

I still like my nostalgic moments, yearnings for a simpler time where success as a collector was all but guaranteed, even if they are only illusory. Most collecting nostalgia is but a fairy tale in which virtue, purity of intention and a clever mind always triumph. If it were only true for any collector knows how unfair the antique gods and goddesses can be. But bemoaning a lost golden age serves a collector ill.

Gatsby in *The Great Gatsby* longs for Daisy but the narrator Nick observes that he cannot repeat the past. A grown-up collector cannot either. He must toss away that fabled innocence, the myths and idealizations, and set aside the charming grief that props up nostalgia. Only then can he be successful in his quest as he prowls show aisles and dealers shops.

Now, if you will excuse me, the fire needs another log or two, and my scotch needs topping off. I will return to the present in a bit.

Nostalgia may blind collectors to the current world of American antiques.

Chapter 7

Passion

Passion – many collectors have it. Some believe it is the engine that keeps the collecting world turning and churning. It certainly leads to a variety of behaviors that those in the non-collecting world might consider unusual, even bizarre. (Of course, passionate love does the same thing.) I think of Brimfield with ankle (heck, thigh) deep mud, rain, and people frantically running hither and yon, smiles on their faces. Wellies on their feet. Dealer vehicles stuck in the mud. They seem oblivious to it all except for the objects they seek. We won't even talk (yes, we will) about waiting in line for hours for a chance, just a chance, to find something that may cost a dearly sum, and this is fun!

Passion – knowing something about it may help us understand our commitment to collecting and explain it to others.

Passion is strong and barely controlled emotion. It is dedication, devotion, intense joy, fervor, spirit, and zeal all rolled into one. To be passionate is to feel alive. Passion needs an object – be it person, hobby, or ideal. Passion is most written about in reference to romance or sexual desire. But interestingly, one can be passionate about just about anything – Star War toys (evoking images and themes from the movies and characters), coins and stamps (beauty, perfection, history to name a few), soccer (sublime motion, a ballet on the pitch), match book covers (geography, war, advertising, hotels, a bygone era), barbed wire (taming the west), license plates (changing eras of automobiles and design), baseball cards (teams, uniforms, unrivaled performance, the American pastime), trivial knowledge (displaying expertise in arcane subjects), chopstick wrappers (you've got me), food labels (consumable goods, changing American style and advertising), and yes, even old stuff we call antiques. Passion is a lamp lit within a person.

We can be passionate to create something – works of art, pottery, delicious food. To be passionate is to devote time and then more time to the object of these intense feelings. We want to, we cannot help ourselves or so it feels. Passion is desire. To understand passion, we must realize it is both an emotion and acts as motivation.

Passion is self-defined. That is why I can be passionate about collecting American antiques and a dear friend can be passionate about writing, and another friend about politics, and my elder son about flying and aviation. But do not make the mistake of equating passion with a visible display of emotion, with histrionics and the like. That stoic New Englander waiting in line with you for a show to open is just as, and perhaps more, passionate about collecting than you. You will find that out when he appears time and time again at shows and auctions you attend, and somehow gets what he is after (just like the handsome cowboy hero gets the girl, or the sheriff gets his man).

Passion is a feeling, so we "feel" passionate about someone or something. But as an emotion it is our thoughts that make sense of and interpret situations or people, informing us that what we are experiencing is desire. Brimfield on a cool, wet May day to a non-collector dragged along by a friend or spouse would not be heavenly. Staying dry and warm, the fatigue – those occurrences and thoughts are not going to lead to a conclusion that what I am experiencing is adventure and passion but rather aversion, a desire to flee, to sit, to get away. In essence we choose to be passionate although in its throes we may be unaware of our thoughts.

To a passionate collector, being cold, wet, and tired at Brimfield is a form of high, a desired and coveted experience. Why would we tolerate it otherwise? Sports fans in Wisconsin well know the experience as they sit in Lambeau Field, in below freezing temperatures with the snow flying,

A Plethora of Feelings

drinking beer, glorifying in the game. To non-Packer fans they are crazed, just as antique collectors' passion probably seems to others. I once stood for five hours in a pub in Southampton England (the Titanic sailed from Southampton on its epic voyage) watching England play in a World Cup soccer game. I am still trying to regain my hearing and sobriety. Oh my, passion in its purest form.

Those who are passionate about collecting antiques may be happy to hear that passion can be an important component in their psychological well-being. For those for whom that is true their collecting passion is considered "harmonious." They can control the passion. It is part of their identity and leads to positive outcomes. They love and value collecting, and the time they invest in it is rewarding. On the other hand, and see if you identify with the following idea, passion also may be considered "obsessive." In the latter case, we cannot control the passion, it contributes to ill- not well-being, and conflicts with other activities. Most collectors define themselves as having harmonious passion yet we all (*don't we?*) know of at least one collector, (and perhaps part of ourselves), who cannot help but add to his collection and is a prisoner of his collecting desires.

The absence of psychological problems does not mean a person's life is "well-lived." He could, for example, feel that he is living a life of quiet desperation, that by conforming he has sold out. His life has no high moments to it. Passion, at least harmonious passion, provides high moments and makes a person feel that life is indeed worthwhile. We engage in happiness-related activities. While tedious I love looking at auction offerings. While I typically do not like to wait in line, I revel in waiting for an antique show to open. While ambiguity at times is difficult for me (need a new password, relationships with others) I love not knowing if I will find something to admire and love at an antique show, or of not knowing if I will be the winning bidder at auction on an item I really want. Welcome to the upside of passion. I know I am not alone in these feelings.

Can one be a truly successful antique collection without passion? An interesting question for which I have no ready answer though I lean toward "no." Passion provides the motivation that propels us to spend large blocks of time (and sometimes money) collecting. Am I as passionate about collecting antiques as I was when I first fell in love as a teenager, or realized I loved the woman to whom I am now married? I do not think so. Just as romantic love over time matures and morphs into what is called "companionate love." I find my collecting passion also has matured, now more of a slow steady red ember burn than a conflagration. Yet it continues to motivate me and collecting continues to be pleasurable and provide meaning in my life.

I cannot find any research on the formation of passion. Why am I passionate about collecting antiques, for example? I have explored the world and find I am not passionate about sports (although I like them), travel (I do like to travel), time with friends (one of my most important activities and I am intentional about getting together with them but would not say I am passionate about friendships) – you get the idea. I theorize that many activities in which we engage prove to be rewarding, but for a variety of reasons (e.g., our personality, what we define as rewarding, being around others who collect) only a few enter the realm of a passion. Maybe, like love with all its passions, how we become passionate for collecting is indeed mysterious.

As a case example of one, always dangerous I know, but I will start with what I know best – myself. I enjoyed antiquing and back roads when I first started collecting. A trip to Colonial Williamsburg was great fun but did not immediately kindle passion. I saw passion role modeled by wonderful dealers who worked with and educated my wife and me. I think their passion was contagious and gave us permission to feel the same. They hoped that we would be antique collectors and build a collection. Anything they suggested seemed rewarding. I liked subscribing to *Ohio Antique Review* and *The Magazine Antiques*, and then *Maine Antique Digest*, and reading them cover to cover. I discovered I loved learning about collecting – objects and their history, dealers and their specialties, and in exploring my own growing tastes and proclivities. I believe that having a wife who shared the collecting journey with me made the kindling of passion easier, although I now am more passionate about collecting than she. Somehow and at some point in time all of those elements ignited into a passion for collecting.

A Plethora of Feelings

As for the formation of passion, it is a question I will pose to collectors in the future when waiting in line at antique shows. Of course, most dealers also are passionate about their careers. I read of one study of 500 college students who had engaged in at least one passionate activity for at least 8.5 hours/week and for six years (on average). The sample is obviously somewhat young, but their passion is already meaningful and long-lasting. Perhaps for genetic and survival reasons as a species we are drawn to passions. It connects us to the world.

While information on how antique collectors became passionate may be somewhat murky (it would be interesting to learn what commonalities our stories share about our collecting passion) I believe that there are common elements in what we are passionate about. These elements include but are not limited to anticipation (Yes, this does sound like a commercial for Heinz ketchup) of the next great find, time with collector friends and "collecting" more of them, the way collecting in so many positive ways passes the time and gives us meaning. Elements of relating old stories and creating new ones, sharing in the positive energy of residents of the collecting universe, continued learning, continuing our love affair in collecting, and waiting, without knowing the outcome, of what next, yet uncollected (by us) genre will make us smile.

An anonymous saying relates, "Purpose is the reason you journey (I could say collect). Passion is the fire that lights the way." Those passionate about collecting feel the passion in their souls. There is almost a religious feeling to the passion collectors experience. They make no apologies for it and why should they? A connoisseur never apologizes for his knowledge or interests. Since we do not know how passion develops perhaps the goal for attracting new collectors to the American antique world would be to have them attend shows, visit dealers or auctions, i.e., be around collectors who are passionate and hope some sustain their interest. Again, I wish I knew more about how passion develops within us as collectors or in other areas of our lives. All I know is that I am thankful for the passions I have, American antiques being near the top of the list.

As for how we lose our passion for collecting antiques, that I can understand. Keep in mind that those collectors we meet and know are a biased sample. By this I mean they are still collecting and probably retain their passion. To understand how passion dims we must return to the idea that it is our thoughts that determine our feelings. I will use a personal example. For over twenty years I volunteered at the "premier" aviation convention. It is the largest of its kind, a national and international gathering of the flying community. I loved the crowds, meeting people (was honored to meet several Tuskegee Airmen just as my wife met many Women Airforce Service Pilots – WASPs), the array of airplanes, the comradery – everything about it. But after a while the week became formulaic. I could predict and anticipate who I would see, what would happen. What I once gloried in as a volunteer was no longer worth the effort. I had burned out on the event. So, I stopped volunteering and attending.

I believe the same process takes place for collectors who lose their passion. It is not that the house is full for there is always room for a piece one loves. It is that collecting no longer creates a "high." The love affair is over. Waiting in line becomes onerous, not wonderful. The crowds become negative, not something to revel in. The collector's behaviors and what he experiences are the same but his thoughts and how he interprets what he is experiencing (his perceptions of collecting) change. Of course, for some, the passion is directed to other outlets, a different form of collecting, travel, volunteer work, cooking, gardening, grandchildren.

But as a life-long collector of antiques I am thankful that the hobby and all I experienced has lasted as long as it has. There is nothing quite like the passion of a collector, whatever his motivation or objects of desire.

The heart needs to attach itself to something outside itself, or it withers.

Chapter 8

Sentimentality

I have talked with this collector many times while we waited in line for shows to open. I did so recently as a matter of fact. And ran into him again in the first hour on a crowded show floor. He was looking at a small (very small actually: inches by inches) piece of embroidery and was thrilled because his mother's first name was stitched in it. I moved on, not knowing if he purchased the piece but the moment stuck with me. I was recently reminded of his discovery when I encountered a piece of redware with writing in slip, "Sarah's Dish." I had never seen this piece of writing before on redware and while the plate's condition was average, I knew I wanted to own it. Sarah is my mother's name and while she has been deceased for some years seeing "her" dish at the show and now as I walk through my home was (is) both powerful and touching.

All of this is preface to an exploration of sentimentality, what it is and how it often plays an important role in the lives of those who collect Americana. A yearning to keep in touch with our past through objects we collect encompasses much more than being a "sentimental fool." I learned, for example, that sentimentality occurs in all age groups and cultures. It must be important, I concluded. I differentiate sentimentality from nostalgia which I discussed in Chapter 6. Nostalgia has a bit more bitterness in it than sentimentality. The latter is a pure recollection of people, places, and events whereas the former is tinged with the belief that things were better in the past. (Some consider the two synonyms whereas I do not.)

Sentimentality is reflective, sweet, and loving. Some people when feeling sentimental tear up, their voices tinged with emotion. When we collect, we can find objects that create a sentimental feeling within us because of their ties to specific events, people, and places in our lives. The antique cookie cutters fill our minds with the smells at holiday time in grandma's kitchen. The ineffable smell that is a combination of fir trees, grass, flowers, and water that rises from the land on the Upper Peninsula in Michigan on an early morning in the summer, as a child romps or walks about. That memory is so intense, important, and positive to my wife decades later that she has instructed that when she dies that her ashes be spread on the creek, as did her uncle, next to the family homestead fields.

Frequently there is a sadness about the loss of these times and people, making sentimentality emotional. Yet when we collect an object that reminds us of them, they are not gone forever. We can remember and live with them still through pieces we felt compelled to purchase. In essence, we keep a tie to our past lives and important people and events through them. Sentimental feelings call up their voice, likeness, and personality. Every time I look at my Sarah's plate, I hear my mother's voice and see her. For a collector, the object precipitating this sentimentality may not have belonged to the person we are remembering, but it somehow evokes them. Perhaps that is why the redware plate with my mother's name is so powerful to me. I speak her name aloud. I think of her – the best of her.

And objects may not just call up sentimental feelings for relatives. Several pieces my wife and I own help me remember dear dealers we bought from long ago. Who knew at the time that they were not only educating and helping us build a collection of high country antiques, but unexpectedly keeping the memory of them alive in us through our antiques? Jim and Bernice Miller specialized, among other things in wooden-works, tall-case clocks. Jim being an engineer could put them in running order, lucky for Bernice. We have three such clocks and when I pull the cords to lift the weights each day, hear the tic-toc as the pendulum swings to and fro, and listen to them strike the hour, I am reminded of

A Plethora of Feelings

what Jim taught me about them, and Bernice's writing another item description and receipt.

In other words, once collectors own certain objects, they become the key that unlocks memories of people, places, and events, and even a motive to reflect on ourselves. We may become wistful and sentimental about our own lives. A dropfront desk in our home reminds me of when my wife and I were first collecting and how young we were back then. I remember how old my children were when we purchased rope beds for them, showing them how to keep the ropes taut (the phrase "sleep tight" originates there). I recall the anxiety of awaiting dealer friends' return from New England laden with treasures to be examined. As I look at our current dining room table, I am brought back to purchasing our first (a country cherry dropleaf) and then our second (a mahogany federal dropleaf) until finally the Queen Anne walnut one graced us with its presence.

Again, there is a tenderness to being sentimental about our lives and those who have entered them. To some, such remembrances may be shallow but so be it. There is room in our lives for such feelings. "A sentimentalist", Oscar Wilde wrote, "is one who desires to have the luxury of an emotion without paying for it." As someone who has lived a relatively long life (truth in disclosure, I am 75 years old) my response to Wilde is simple. "I have paid enough over the years, so leave me some moments of uninterrupted sentimentality." I take my occasional soppy feelings with gratitude.

When I have viewed others' collections, the pieces their attention lingered on were not necessarily the best, not the *10s*. They were the ones with the best stories or that evoked memories they cherished. The antique show where the chair was purchased is described in idyllic terms (and what the collector paid for it seems more fantasy than truth to me). The dealer who sold them the clock was a wonderful person with a keen eye, all of which may be true, but I detect sadness in the collector's voice. The dealer is deceased. The shop where the table was found was a wonderful place, as well it may have been, but there is a wistfulness in the collector's voice, as we mutually mourn the shops that we used to spend time in that no longer exist.

Sentimentality

Sentimentality lets us escape the literal boundaries of time and space. I not only touch our nearly 300-year-old dining room table with awe of what it has seen and heard, one way of traveling through time, but I know where it was crafted in New England, kindling memories of my numerous trips to a part of the country I love so.

Another type of sentimentality calls up special people in our lives because the object in question is one that they once owned themselves. The object connects us with them. An article in *Maine Antique Digest* contains a wonderful description of this form of sentimentality.

> But the buyer wasn't bidding on the strength of the possible artist's name. She acquired it [painting of kittens studying a moth] because it was a cherished family heirloom that had once hung in her grandmother's home. 'The name means absolutely nothing to me,' she smiled through tears of joy for her acquisition. (December 2019, p, 52)

I identify with her happiness. In purchasing this treasure, she had regained part of her and her grandmother's life. The painting will now be an excuse, when the mood strikes her, to keep her relationship with her grandmother alive. Perhaps that is one reason the folklore says that collecting a specific genre skips a generation. That which I collect does not interest my children but may interest my grandchildren. If true, perhaps it is they who need the sentimentality of a time (to them) long ago.

Sentimentality also allows collectors to escape from humdrum lives, the absurdities we must accept. How very strange, yet wonderful, the tenderness that small piece of embroidery evoked in the collector with whom I had talked. It was as if, for the moment, he was transported, oblivious to the hustle and bustle around him. He had found his mother's name, and through the small piece of material had found her as well, and what can be more important than that? The redware plate with my mother's name reminds me of her life and mine, both of our journeys, giving me an identity and my life a narrative. Those thoughts and feelings take me far from mundane and dreary tasks or people in my life.

But I know from personal experience that not every object from

A Plethora of Feelings

one's family that might yield tears of joy does so, although I am at a loss to describe why some do and some do not. We are not sentimental about everything. My father's parents emigrated from Russia to the United States. One of the family necessities they brought with them was a samovar. How they transported it all those miles in one piece is beyond me. It sat for years in my parents' dining room. I had the opportunity to become its caretaker and declined the honor. My brother now enjoys it. Despite my love for my grandparents and parents, the positive memories associated with them, the samovar failed to touch me, It brought no tears of joy. Sentimentality, I conclude, is selective. Despite monetary value or artistic merit, some objects fail to elicit it. My wife and I have one painting my parents enjoyed. It is of a pub in Cornwall England, built in the 13th century. A wonderful story accompanies it. When I look at it, I can see their condominium where they lived for so many years after my father retired and see other paintings besides it. Sentimentality personified.

I did something I had never done before. It was quiet day. I took a deep breath, and mug of tea in hand, as ready for the memories as I was ever going to be, I walked through our house, looking at our antiques from a sentimental perspective. (I am sure leisurely staring at a wall of family photographs would serve the same purpose.) While many pieces took me back years or decades, only a few elicited reminiscences. And for those that did, the experience was indeed intense. The jelly cupboard in refrigerator-white paint my wife and I, when so very young, took down to the cherry wood underneath. My wife's Howdy Doody set of marionettes (complete with background and original box) evokes in her a longing for the innocence of childhood. The bowl and pitcher I purchased for her as a wedding present (we now have been married over 50 years) takes me back to relative youth, romantic love, and when my life opened before (rather than behind) me. The Tuskegee airmen poster, *Keep up Flying! Buy War Bonds* reminds me and my wife of their sacrifice. We met many of these airmen over the years and now almost all are deceased. My silver baby cup hangs in the kitchen. A basket of my wife's toys from 70 years ago sits under a window. How could one not become sentimental? The list goes on.

In brief, being sentimental serves many purposes. It preserves innocence. A certain type of summer day reminds me of being a child, lying on the backyard lawn, staring at the clouds just as the smell of certain foods reminds me to this day of being a child. Being sentimental also connects. Just as the painting of kittens connects the granddaughter with her grandmother, objects that surround me connect me with friends from long ago. Finally, sentimentality gives our lives continuity and meaning. It can intensify our mood.

Some doubt our hobby of collecting, or mock it, not understanding the riches it provides to our daily lives. They fail to understand it is our way of adding depth and texture to being, often through the sentimentality it allows. It shores us up against loss and aging, protects us, and nurtures us and others. If collecting did nothing else, it would still be a valuable pursuit.

Our minds live in an unending past. Nothing disappears completely. All dwells in aura.

Chapter 9

Trust (Faith) and the American Antique World

There it is a gorgeous piece at the show. You are falling in love before even taking a closer gander. It wasn't on your list of pieces to look for, but love is love. The price seems fair although it is expensive for your pocketbook. You talk with the dealer, you look at it a bit more, you put a hold on it to walk around the show and clear your head. You return and purchase the item. What just happened?

Well, obviously you trusted your eye, and your trusted your feelings, that "blink" moment. But you also (without sufficient data) decided that you would trust the dealer. You had followed this dealer at shows and on his website but had never purchased from him. Your conversation with him about the piece seemed okay. He was knowledgeable, did not pressure you to buy, told you about the best he could do on price. In retrospect, you trusted yourself and him, and wrote out the check. Trust, formed over time with the dealer from a distance (not the best way to assess someone) and affirmed in just a few minutes at the show.

Having written about collectors and hope, it is time to put pen to paper and discuss collectors' faith. (Perhaps I will find a way to also, at some point in time write about charity, the greatest of the three great virtues according to Apostle Paul that the New Testament calls for.) Faith is a trust or confidence in someone or something. In religion it is a strong belief in God or a religion's doctrines, not based on proof but on spiritual trust. For our purposes if you "have faith" in someone that means that you trust that person. Faith can be thought of as having three components: the emotional, the cognitive, and the practical. Let's take a closer look at trust and its importance for collectors. Hope (Chapter 5) emphasizes the future, trust lives in the here and now.

To have faith in someone is to depend on them, to be able to predict their behavior and find it to your liking. You can know that someone is a scoundrel, that at every turn he will turn to deceit and lies as he describes and tries to sell you an antique. But simply because you can predict his behavior does not mean you trust him. Trust implies a "leaning on," a meaningful relationship. Trust, like hope, is a fuel that powers the buying and selling of antiques.

While some may view trust as naïve, gullible, and doomed many psychological theorists posit it is a basic human motivation and adaptive for the species. It would be difficult for humans to live or work in groups without trust. Believe it or not, most people are basically trusting and have a bias to trust others, making the violation of our trust so painful, and the giving up of trust sometimes so difficult. At the same time psychologists posit that we must be vigilant (watchful) for indicators of broken trust if we are to thrive. Trust, then, is central to human relationships. Part of resilience for any person, and for our purposes, dealer or collector, is the formation of new trust after one's trust in someone has been broken.

Trust is hard won. It takes time and many interactions to learn that someone is true to a code of ethics, true to his word. Trust also is easily lost – one duplicity, the feeling of being lied to, one piece inaccurately described – and a dealer, picker, auctioneer, collector – can feel like a fool, vowing never to do business with the big talking conjurer again. So, we will look for someone else on whom to rely, who is reliable and steadfast, who is able and truthful. To have confidence in someone, to believe in them, is a feeling made up of numerous interactions. At the end of these encounters, you conclude, often unconsciously, that you trust this person, and this is what you tell yourself.

Unfortunately, once you trust someone you may explain away statements and behaviors that would cause another person, new to a relationship with this dealer, for example, to doubt his truthfulness. To move from trust to distrust causes dissonance. We may feel foolish to have been taken in, we may begin to doubt ourselves, embarrassed to share we were taken advantage of. Even knowing that the formation of trust is never 100 percent foolproof, we want to believe in ourselves, our judgment of others, and in the people around us. But to hang onto trust for too long can cause a collector financial pain, and perhaps stuck with objects that he not only overpaid for, but which are not as represented (see Chapter 2).

Some collectors are surprised to realize that dealers must also trust them. When you tell a dealer that you are looking for wonderful silver tongs for asparagus or sugar, she needs to know that if she finds such pieces, you will seriously consider them, and over time purchase from her. Otherwise, she is wasting her time. Once you have agreed on a price for a piece a dealer needs to know you will pay in a timely manner, or over time as agreed upon. Dealers need customers (clients) to be good to their word. Dealers need to depend on collectors building collections as they have discussed. Collectors who continually change their mind, one minute seeking silver, the next ceramics, and the next paintings wear a dealer out. They cannot depend on the collector's interest. If a dealer who sells a great deal on-line and who asks for payment before shipment, breaks his rule, and the client reneges, argues about price, and so forth, the dealer will probably never sell to that collector again. Why bother if the collector's word is no good.

Auction houses also need to establish trust in the marketplace, among dealers and collectors alike. Stating that an auction house philosophy is "buyer beware "(*caveat emptor*) and then continually misdescribe pieces up for auction or carry goods that have extensive restoration with no statement as such, will eventually cause potential bidders to go elsewhere. Yes, doing business in that manner may be an avenue to immediate success, but in the long run the house's reputation will suffer, people will know and whisper. Of course, the auctioneers may not care about reputation. They may agree with P. T. Barnum although there is no demonstrable proof that he ever made the statement, "There's a sucker (fool) born every minute."

Clinically, those who prey on others, who deceive, are masters at establishing trust and then dissembling if confronted about their lack of honesty. They always have reasonable explanations, always can still the waters, leave the person being deceived feeling satisfied. And we like to believe that we are good judges of others' character. Or that we are special. Surely Mr. Smith would not treat me the way I heard he treated Mr. Jones. I am one of his best customers. The need to feel special, to feel good about ourselves can get in the way of honest relationships with others.

Here is a time when it is helpful for a collector to talk with others although dealers may be hesitant to label a fellow dealer as a schnook or worse, a crook. Sometimes the marketplace is like the United States Senate and the "esteemed" dealers may band together. But if you get to know some dealers well, hopefully they will politely and quietly steer you away from those you should not trust. And collectors in my experience will be forthcoming about which dealers they trust and whom they will not buy from.

Trust does not imply perfection. Dealers may not have had time to give every piece they sell a complete looking at. Auction houses may make mistakes in attribution or condition, sometimes to collectors' advantages if they know what they are _really_ bidding on. I remember purchasing a piece of painted tin I learned was fake, the pattern had never been applied to the form in question according to an expert I know. The dealer from whom I purchased the piece took it back quickly and apologized. My wife and I own a wonderful tiger maple chest of drawers purchased from dealers we trusted and from whom we made many purchases. The top (a gorgeous piece of tiger maple with a deep thumbnail molding) is a replacement and it probably took as much time to pick out the piece of tiger maple for the replacement top as it did to make the original. The dealers had purchased the chest early in their careers; they increased their expertise over time. My wife and I still have the chest, for even with the newer top it is too good and has too many memories to sell. Our trust in these dealers was not shaken.

Of course, there are ways to behaviorally deal with issues of getting taken. I have told others I would never go to Brimfield and spend serious dollars without someone more knowledgeable than I to accompany me. I feel the same way about purchasing an expensive piece at auction. I simply do not trust my knowledge enough. I need help and expertise. Collectors should heed and listen to disquieting interactions with dealers or auction houses even though the feeling is probably uncomfortable. If a collector can put into words what is causing the uneasiness and reflect on the unlistened to clues, he may well arrive at the conclusion that the party in question behaved in distrustful ways. It sometimes takes effort and patience to realize the full truth of the homily, "Fool me once, shame on you, fool me twice, shame on me."

The reality or problem with trust is that it cannot be avoided. Trust is central to relationships. We need to trust. It makes the world right, both the feeling and the conscious decision that someone can be trusted. Yet the formation of trust can be mysterious. Do we consciously estimate the number of interactions with someone and the probability that they can be depended on, time after time? I do not believe so. Instead, we find ourselves trusting someone, hopefully knowing that the trust is not absolute, but tied to specific situations. I may trust an antique dealer to be honest with me but may not put my life in his hands. That is what loved ones and dear friends are for.

And which comes first, the feeling that I can trust someone else, or a positive feeling for someone that precedes my trust in him? Does liking lead to trust or does trust lead to liking? Or is that the wrong question. For you can trust a curmudgeonly dealer but not like him or her. And you can like someone but know full well they are not dependable, are not to be trusted.

Quite a conundrum. We have a basic need to trust, to do so is adaptive for our well-being yet at the same time trust carries risks. We can be deceived, let down, financially ripped off, and the like. Yet I concur with Hemingway that "The best way to find out if you can trust somebody is to trust them." Do so with good data, however. One interaction or transaction with someone, unless fraught with difficulty and many levels of trust, is insufficient to form a good conclusion that someone is trustworthy. Typically, it takes multiple interactions over time to lead to a valid conclusion that one's trust in someone else is warranted. And while it may be simplistic, use another's actions as a basis for trust, not his words. If he follows up honestly on his words that is one thing. But words can be easily spoken and bely trust at every opportunity.

As important as trust is, I have seldom heard it discussed by collectors. It is as if bringing up issues of trust taints the entire American antiques marketplace, dirties it in some way. Yet the few times I have asked collectors if there were dealers at an antique show from whom they would not buy, I am often surprised about the well-formed opinions I heard and reasons for these opinions.

Interpersonally trust is the gold standard in collecting. It builds bonds that are deep and can be permanent. It leads to collections built and money made. I often wondered if the scions of the antique world, both dealers and auction houses, became so not necessarily because of longevity in the business, or their eye, but because of trust. If that was not the reason, it should have been. I hope your trust is well-founded and others' trust in you the same. For Anton Chekhov was correct when he stated that "You must trust and believe in people or life becomes unbearable."

Ironically and importantly, to collect successfully, you must trust others just as you yourself must be trustworthy.

Section II

A Tasteful Indulgence
(Most of the Time)

Chapter 10

Color

"Color is the place where our brain and the universe meet."
Paul Klee

Recently, while watching our city's Memorial Day Parade I was struck by the riot of color. Lots of red, white, and blue, of course, but also a colorful blur of spectators. Middle and high school students wore black uniforms or outfits and the brass section glimmered and blinked. Veterans were natty in their dress blue or army green uniforms. While a somber holiday the parade was uplifting, the colors carried the feeling, which got me thinking about American decorative arts and color.

If one reads about such matters as interior decoration, colors make or break a design. While mavens insist, we can learn to pick the perfect colors for our tastes and occasions, they also lecture us on learning the basics of the color wheel, the use of neutrals, contrasts, clashes, and the various types of color schemes. Still, like everything else, taste is subject to change and fads. Interiors become dated partially because of the colors used. Annually one or more new "in" colors are trumpeted. I do hope that Fiesta-orange shag carpeting never returns, but the trend from white to gray to pale colors to bold statements seems caught in an endless cycle. Pantone Color Institute announces the color of the year, influencing what we think makes our interiors look fresh and modern. (If you are interested, Pantone's 2018 Color of the Year is ultra-violet, a bright, highlighter hue. In 2021 it was ultimate gray. As an aside, I have no idea what a highlighter hue is.) Where all this agonizing led me is the simple question: Wouldn't it be interesting if every few years the antique world selected a new "in" color and we had to revise our collections to be *au courant*, or *au fait* or . . . I am tempted to add aw shucks. Time to find Windsor chairs in ultra-violet. Oy vey!

No question, our upbringing and life experiences influence our color preferences. We find blue soothing because that was the hue of our favorite blankie, red exciting like that Radio Flyer wagon we played with as a child. Colors influence how much we like certain foods and scientists say color can even affect whether some placebos (all sugar pills mind you) work better than others.

A walk through any antique show brings to life antiques and their vibrancy – the faded or glimmering pieces, a sea of tones. My experience tells me that collectors care about color, care intensely. Color is one of the key variables when purchasing furniture and many other antiques. Many collectors seek original paint since the wearing evokes a history and narrative about the antique. Canadian antique furniture comes in amazing colors. Color pleases the eye and creates enjoyment. And personal factors, our own tastes, and inclinations (the source of which we may sometimes be unaware of), determine the antiques (and their colors) we are drawn to.

I write from a naïve perspective. I have never used an interior decorator in building or displaying my collection. One does not often hear a begrudging, "I got tired of the blue blanket chest because I wanted a red one that went with the new wallpaper." Nonetheless I hardly hesitate to candidly admit that I would sell our Tracy brace back Windsor chairs (in original black) if I found an equal pair (in form and originality) in original green. They would cost more too: Color affects value. Certainly, collectors are drawn to a particular palate of colors in the chests, chairs, fabrics that cover their chairs and sofas, and in their paintings, quilts, and earthenware.

Seeing antiques in color on dealer websites and in publications grants them a life black-and-white cannot capture. Some of the items in the color photos stand out from the page. Imagine the furniture in Fales and Bishop's *American Painted Furniture: 1660-1880*, pictured in color photos, rendered instead in black and white. Paint was used to both "preserve and embellish." Original hues give a sense of life, depth, and history. Until I started thinking about antiques and color, I was hardly aware of how vibrant the interior of our home is made by the presence of what we have gathered – this even though the occasional visitor remarked on the riot of tints that caught his or her attention.

A Small Study

As a social scientist, my inclination is to collect data from a host of dealers and collectors on their preferences for antiques in certain colors and then, generalize from what I have learned. Lacking such data, I must perforce use a small sample of these folks. Let's see how their normal (or so I flatter myself thinking) minds work. I asked them what objects came immediately to mind when they thought of a color, or if they thought of a specific object, and whether the color was a favorite. Compare their responses with yours. (A warning, they often have exquisite and expensive taste.)

White:

A rare color in painted American furniture. An example is provided by early 19th C. wedding-band hogscraper candle sticks. One respondent owns a Queen Anne chair in original white, a favorite piece. White is her best-loved color because of its rarity. Another immediately thought of Robert Sack's Willard wedding clock that sold for $744,000 in 2006. You could label the color a scrubbed-top tavern-table white, but is it really? Homespun blankets often have white threads. But as a primary flourish or ornamentation the color white is rare.

Blue:

Take for example an 18th century firkin and an 18th century blanket chest, both in robin's egg blue. Jim Grievo's Stedman Ovid, Eagle Incised Jug (sold at Pook and Pook), $402,900.

New Haven, Connecticut incised stoneware jug, ca. 1825-1830, by Absalom Stedman, with incised cobalt decorated spread winged American eagle with shield breast holding an American flag in one talon and arrows in the other, a cloud like banner arises from the eagle's beak, incised. Made by A. Stedman, 19 1/4" h. Exhibited: Abby Aldrich, Williamsburg, Virginia, October 12, 1975. Provenance: Preston Bassett collection; Barry Cohen; David Schorsch; Fred Giampetio.

Blue is a most (<u>the most?</u>) desirable color. Dealers scrape cupboards and blanket chests down to the original blue. Some blue darkens with age, while robin's-egg seems to soften and seduce. Blue shows up in quilts, 18th century coverlets, and homespun. Delftware (blue and white) is common. Painted firkins and boxes are stacked. My wife and I cannot be the only collectors of Bennington pottery in its well-known and -liked blue color.

Red:

Red paint or wash graces 18th century Queen Anne tables and William and Mary blanket chests, furniture, and painted boxes. I conclude red was in high demand when the objects were crafted. Redware wears its name proudly. I find an old red, softened with age (a nice way of saying faded, perhaps) peaceful.

Yellow:

Yellow crops up on chairs circa 1830-1850 with painted or stenciled backs, dressing tables, 19th century cutlery boxes, and Sgraffito ware (an earthenware). One dealer was captivated by the yellow slip decoration on a plate pictured in *Seeing Red: Southeastern Pennsylvania Earthenware from Winterthur*. The plate, made in 1785 is described as follows:

> This redware dish, attributed to George Hubener, has all the bells and whistles collectors want. The bold sgraffito tulip design on a yellow ground is accented with green splotches, and the German inscription includes the date 1785. The example, similar to

one in the Winterthur collection, sold at Pook & Pook in January 2008 for $351,000, a redware record.

Shaker furniture was sometimes yellow (full disclosure: my wife and I own none). It is seen on painted boxes, and in the slip providing decoration on redware, as noted. Yellow ware pottery and spongeware provide frequent, sometimes striking examples. There also is the color ochre, a light brownish yellow.

Gold:
Gold leaf was applied to weathervanes and traces often can still be seen. Sometimes older furniture was "updated" in the 1830s or so, by applying gold paint for decoration (one of our tall case clocks has such striping on a plain black case and a set of our chairs shed golden "teardrops"). Gold frames are common around paintings and coruscates on old clock dials.

Black:
This is hardly a rare tone in 17th and early 18th century chairs and other furniture. My wife and I own a tall case clock with a painted black case. The asphaltum base on painted tin is black. In paintings, we see it on the hull of a schooner cutting through the water.

Bittersweet, Salmon, or Pumpkin:
Bittersweet, halfway between red and yellow, and pumpkin hues show up in 18th century whole cloth (commonly called Linsey-woolsey), pantry boxes, cupboards, and chests. One respondent loves a basket painted bittersweet and sporting robin's egg blue trim.

Green:
This color is often found on the most desirable redware, Windsor chairs, cupboards, weathervanes, and quilts.

Silver:
Is the color of solder used on tin. It is the natural hue of coin sil-

ver spoons and mustard ladles (my wife has a small collection) and, of course, sterling silver and pewter goods (silver gray).

Brown:

This may be the most common color encountered by collectors of early American furniture. Examples include 18th century treenware, brown or Spanish brown furniture (the latter a dark reddish brown). A Queen Anne drop leaf table we own is so dark that it approaches black. Unpainted furniture adds a variety of hues and shades to a room and is not necessarily dull or boring. A homespun blanket in browns is unusual, probably early, and quite pretty.

Polychrome:

The rainbow was not ignored by our ancestors, nor is it unknown in their collectibles. We see it in Pennsylvania blanket chests, works of art, and vintage posters. Painted clock dials often display several colors, the panoply adding to the delight of pictured flowers, fruit, or birds. Shirred and braided rugs, antique toys and game boards also host a multitude of hues. Containing black, gold, white, blues, and pink among others we own a marine painting:

> Circa 1840-1860 ship portrait, two-masted schooner, the E. A. Elliott. American, probably coastal New England. Unsigned, attributed to Elisha Baker or James Babbidge. Oil on canvas, original frame. 23 3/8" X 31 3/8". Excellent condition, lightly cleaned, otherwise untouched.

Where Else We Find Color

It appears on the walls and floors of homes. Even more than 200 years ago, not all surfaces were whitewashed. Mount Vernon's walls have color everywhere. The wallpaper early Americans purchased from England or France was bold in color and often patterned. The fact is, while so many pictured early American as a monochromatic world, our ancestors liked color and were not timid in its use. Stenciled murals (Rufus Porter comes to mind) are now muted and beautiful, but they were originally bright and bold, and yes, beautiful. Stencil designs appeared on walls and floors (on oriental, penny, or braided rugs).

Musings on Color

I have never seen research exploring the color preferences of antique collectors and I am at a loss to explain my own. I walked through our home looking only at color, not form, scale, and the like. It was like seeing our collection anew and I urge you to give it a try.

The antique I most wish we would have purchased and did not was robin's egg blue (a blanket chest). I once passed on a Windsor bench with wonderful form because it had no paint (no color). We have never thought of painting the interior walls of our home anything but white. We would rather let our collection speak for itself. Nonetheless, the trim in our rooms is painted different colors and the stairwell walls wear wallpaper in a large pattern. I have no idea what a decorator would think of all the colors in our home, but I am not sure I would much care. I am drawn to several depictions of Blacks from *Harpers Weekly* that we framed and hung, though the drawings are not tinted.

This dialogue with color has taught me not only about what I like but why I (we) collect what I do. I shall continue asking my fellow collectors and dealers about their color preferences and see what I learn (oh, how I hope I find I am as normal as I think). The artist Edvard Munch once said, "The colors live a remarkable life of their own after they have been applied to the canvas."

Antique hues evoke the past and the delights hues brought to daily life in a bygone era. For many collectors color is the *sine qua non* of what they collect.

Chapter 11

Condition

The clarion call resounds throughout the Americana collecting world. "Condition is everything" echoes in every antique buyer's mind. Hence, buying the best you can afford becomes both a mantra and a corollary. Now condition may be "everything" but the more I looked at collecting in general and my own collecting in particular, the more I began to distrust what I thought of as the "condition bromide." The concept and its assumed absolute worth are much more nuanced than I originally believed.

With the recent devastating fire at Notre Dame Cathedral in Paris, many learned for the first time the numerous occasions the building had been added to, rebuilt, and restored. Already fierce discussions rage about its steeple and what its replacement "should" or "must" look like. Will the alleged purity, authenticity, or similarity to past exemplars in any of the restoration work make Notre Dame less sacred or less important to people? I seriously doubt it. Witness the example of the "Salvator Mundi" painting from the hand of Leonardo (maybe) that brought over $400 million dollars at auction. Numerous pundits and art experts noted that there was little left of Leonardo's original work after so many centuries of in-painting and restoration. But the artwork was so rare as to be both irresistible and precious.

At a more approachable level, the condition of the pieces we collect can be thought of as having many shades, and the meaning of condition – at least on an absolute scale – substantially differs from one collector to the next. One man's trash is another's treasure, or so the cliché has it, and the assertion is no less valid simply because it has become a truism.

To buttress that bold assertion, I bear witness to my own collecting. A dropfront desk graces our living room – a desk on frame with Queen Anne legs. The hinges are not original but that is acceptable A large round ink stain marks its lid when open. Seemingly, this diminishes the piece. In fact, it does not, for one subtle fragment of condition is individual taste. To a purist for whom condition is his most important criterion, the ink stain is jarring, a sign the desk does not meet his elevated standards. To me the ink stain is a source of delight. It is a sign of human intervention in a material world. The desk has been used over the centuries and its appearance speaks of its age. Seeing the mark, I ask myself, Who knocked over the inkwell? Why is the stain round? Could it not be mopped up? The item remains silent, of course, but the desk's very flaw is not a flaw at all. It involves me in it, in its past, in its worldly function.

Evidence of material culture, use over the years in many cases, presents a superb example of the significance and worth of condition. Speaking for myself, if I wanted a piece to look new, shiny, and unmarked, I would purchase a reproduction of an antique. Instead, I respect and like signs that an old piece is gracefully getting on in years. A pair of bannister-back chairs in my collection also come to mind. Their paint is crusty, and the rush seats show their use. Victorian gold striping was added in the early 19th century. Somehow this adds a sort of raffish flavor to them, even though they are hardly in the condition they were when they left the hand of the craftsman who made them. Yet I prefer them to examples I have seen at auction, gleaming as if they had recently left the woodworker's shop. Such is the power of individual taste in assessing the worth of a particular piece.

At the same time, I do not like pieces that are too "primitive," studded with wormholes, for example. Confronted with this preference I pause and wonder, What then does condition mean to me? It was a good question when it first intruded in my mind and one I am still pondering.

A Tasteful Indulgence

Evidently, I will accept and even cherish evidence of time's interference . . . but not too much of it.

If I contemplate purchasing a piece the experts have decreed flawed by too much restoration, I need powerful reasons to do so, regardless of its cost.

In the main, the effect of different levels of condition on the desirability and worth of a piece is decided by those said to be in the know, the cognoscenti. Levels of condition are their dicta. How these arcane classifications are determined, however, is a bit mysterious. There is no annual "What condition is okay?" forum I am aware of. But the acceptability of condition is decided upon, nonetheless. Ended-out feet on a 17th or early 18th century chair are now acceptable (They were not always. See below). Replaced hinges on my drop front desk are similarly decreed in bounds, as is the cleaning of a painting if done professionally and lightly. Repairing a piece of redware in minor ways gets the expert's nod. And the chorus of "okays" sings out in many more ways than my few examples offer. Some collectors march to their own drummers, ignoring the expert opinions and prejudices and are only satisfied with the most pure and untouched of pieces. Others gravitate in the opposite direction, perhaps valuing ornamentation, rarity, attribution, or proportion equally with or over a piece's condition.

But I remembered that someone had laid out the base commandments of condition and I found the encyclical – no not a letter sent out by a bishop to the pope but close. Albert Sack in the 1960 book *Fine Points of Furniture – Early American* includes a chapter titled "Restorations, Replacements and Imperfections" that makes for fascinating reading. Sack divides restorations on 17th and 18th century furniture into "major" and "minor." A major restoration eliminates the piece from a "discriminating" collector's consideration, making the piece worth less. A minor restoration affects neither the piece's value nor its aesthetic credentials. Sack also notes any changes to pieces are evaluated by dealers and collectors alike. He anticipates disagreements with his taxonomy. He falls back on his guiding principles: Is the piece "well preserved" and from an "important school of American craftsmanship?"

For today's collector a few examples from Sack's thinking illustrate the many shades of condition he endorses or denigrates. Loss of feet to a bureau, a replaced top or later embellishments are "major" changes in condition. The same holds true for ended-out chair or desk legs, the replacement of a Windsor stretcher, a married (the top and bottom did not begin life together) chest-on-chest, a replaced dial on a tall-case clock. The list goes on and on. I wonder, some 60 years later, how much more tolerant Albert Sack would be today – since what he considers fine pieces are more difficult to find, – and how his list would differ were he alive to update it? Notice that replaced hinges on a desk are not listed as major, and he does not deal with issues of surface, except to note an original patina adds greatly to a piece's desirability and worth. But doesn't French polishing, which I believe the Sack firm used, retain a piece's patina while adding a smooth surface? Today such restoration would be frowned upon by many collectors.

Weathervanes provide another example of the fluid nature of condition assessments. At some point in time "good condition" required such an object have no or only very few bullet holes. Then, weathervanes gained cachet as works of art, sculptures to be appreciated for their aesthetics. Bullet holes (unless too numerous) were no longer major impediments to desirability. Perhaps "Foresight, Hindsight, Point of View" in the book, *A Collection of American Folk Art Sculpture* (1998) most vividly illustrates the change. Weathervanes are "sculpture" with all the grace and movement great sculpture has, despite the loss of arms, feet, and other parts often present. Weathervanes we are told are art to be appreciated for their aesthetic value: "classic forms that are joyful, powerful, beautiful, generally curvilinear in nature, sometimes playful and whimsical . . ." It is these attributes that become paramount, superseding other elements in assessing the piece's quality, not what would ordinarily be thought of as conditional faults.

Let us also not ignore rarity as a potent determinant of a piece's value. A collector is putting together a small collection of redware plates with writing on them. (Truth, that is me.) Such pieces used to be relatively common but are now more difficult to find. I come across a piece with a woman's name I have never seen before in this genre. The plate is amazingly inexpensive. Why? Sold by a well-known auction house, the plate was accurately described as having "extensive" restoration. The dealer who has it for sale was honest about its condition: From a distance it looks fine but upon close inspection one can tell it has been reassembled and the glaze worked on. Such remedial work is not inexpensive, so someone at some point in time thought enough of the piece, or the profit to be made from it, justify the work done. Those who deal in and collect ceramics have arrived at their own conclusions. The cosmetic restoration done to this redware plate affects its integrity, desirability, and financial value. Even so, it is rare. A search through past auctions of Americana revealed no other similar pieces bearing the same name. And it is very affordable. Yet I hesitate. What would it mean to have this redware plate in my collection? How would I feel about it? Would its rarity supersede its evidently poor condition prior to its restoration? Should I purchase it?

I can tell you that the choice I confront is a lonely one, for it is entirely mine. No dealer, and I talked with a few, can give me a definitive answer. Instead, they lay out the issues involved on the plus and minus side of the purchase equation. I know that dealers point to a piece's condition (when it is good) as a positive attribute of the antique, a reason to purchase it. Because of what the cognoscenti have decreed and the *zeitgeist* of condition, most dealers are picky about the condition of Americana they purchase for sale. At the same time, knowing that many dealers have at home pieces they decided to keep because they simply like them, even though at times their rough condition precludes their sale, I lean toward purchasing this redware plate. I do acknowledge the dollars it costs me could go toward a "better" (perhaps more accurately, a "different") piece. That, too, is my condition conundrum.

If you were to tell someone that collecting is sometimes a wrestling match, you might get interesting looks in return. But that is what I am mentally doing here – wrestling with condition versus rarity. In talking with other collectors, I find that I am not alone in grappling with such tradeoffs. One dealer with whom I talked characterized the dilemma as "passion versus comfort" and he was quite evidently familiar with it. Will knowing the plate is exceedingly rare make me comfortable in owning it, even though it is in markedly poorer condition than others in my collection? Will my passion for collecting redware overcome my doubts? I might add there is another variable in play. I may never see another plate with this name on it. So why wait? I agonize that its condition might bother me. When I look at it, will I smile or feel the fool?

The same dealer who talked about tradeoffs noted that condition issues simply "bug some people." He asked whether it would bug me. Will I see what is there or what is not there? I do not know the answer right now. Perhaps my passion to add to my collection will be stronger than the small devil whispering in my other ear, "the condition, the condition."

Another dealer with whom I spoke offered what I took to be a consolation:

> Condition is just another fashionable buzzword. It is a matter of fact that it did not hold the weight at one time that it does today (think the value of a Chippendale chest with replaced feet in 1970 vs. today). Tomorrow it may not hold the weight it does today.

What I take from this statement is that my collection is personal and thus unique. If I feel I must apologize for this plate's condition (or that of any piece in my collection) I am conceding that I made a mistake in purchasing it. I must have the courage of my conviction, be brave in expressing my taste and aesthetic values (we are back to courage again) – maybe steal from that old phrase and march to my own collector drummer. Since dollars are not a primary consideration, love must be granted a role. I will have to follow my heart. Yet at this moment, I have still not made the decision. Perhaps I am taking too much pleasure in the process, even though I concede it cannot go on forever.

When it comes to the place of judging the importance of condition, I believe that there are no hard and fast rules. Dealers can offer advice as to what bits and pieces added to or lacking from furniture, ceramics, weathervanes, paintings, samplers, or whatever affect a piece's desirability. But a collector cannot overlook the simplest facts. First, antiques are old and that means they have undergone transitions forced upon them by the passage of time. They are not new household goods, but when they were they were lived with and on, and in. Second, collectors do not primarily pursue and obtain pieces to make money when the antiques are sold. Collecting is not an investment, but a hobby. At the same time, collecting is not a charity; informed and wise decisions are both needed and valued. And then there is what I believe are the most important things in making a decision: How I feel and what I see when I look at a piece – its faults viewed with a frown, or its merits viewed with a smile?

There is something instructive about the great Notre Dame fire. The decorative tower that might and might not be replaced may look to some as embodying the character of the cathedral, may seem to be a part of its grace and excellence. Still, it was a cosmetic addition to the original structure, a rather late one at that.

Each collector must decide the meaning of a piece's condition when considering and purchasing items for his collection.

Chapter 12

The Psychology of a Well-Designed Show Booth

The story is told and regularly repeated. In old-time antique dealers' shops collectors had to work to find the best. Dealers would put precious pieces in the back of cupboards or hide them in corners. I do not know if such is the case today but reading again about how dealers used to make collectors work to find the best got me thinking about today's antique shops and even more so of their show booths . . . and what I like and do not like in their layout and design.

Let me for the moment examine what I see as the psychology behind, and complexities involved in staging a "wow!" booth and offer some opinions along the way.

I find it does not matter whether a show has just opened, and its floor and booths are crowded or if it is a lazy late afternoon and all is quiet. A well-designed booth is exactly that. The person who has put it together has, intentionally or accidentally, mastered the psychology of display and merchandising. The visual merchandising literature presents some common elements of presentation done well, and while you and I may differ at times about what it says, I bet your tastes and proclivities share common elements with mine.

A dealer I know thought that the contrasting poles of booth design are business and art, with most dealers falling in the middle. I am not clear one can so easily separate the two when it comes to a well-designed booth, though generally speaking presentation (art) may increase interest in its antiques and sales (business).

Visual Merchandising

When the first department stores such as Chicago's Marshall Field's began merchandising directly to the public, visual displays of goods became crucial. These arrangements appeared both in the store windows and within the store. Visual merchandising's goal was and is supposed to attract customers and increase sales. Visual merchandising can become a brand for a store (or antique booth). Certainly, anyone who shops at the same venue over time, if asked, could describe the recurring display themes. The difficulty is that a "brand" may eventually become stale or clichéd. A seller's eternal problem is how to differentiate his or her store or antique booth from competitors'. In essence visual merchandising demands creating an inviting environment.

Antique collectors may be familiar with the words "sales environment" but in my experience seldom use the term. An antique show has its own visual culture, its own ambiance – the use of tables, floor covering, temporary walls, lighting, flowers and plants, spots where food and beverage is available, sometimes music with its own tempo, character, and appeal. Within this environment each individual antique dealer's booth creates its own mini environment. All sellers have the same goal: to sell its product, and to reflect the personality and tastes of the dealer, hoping these resonate with potential customers. The psychology behind visual merchandising is to fashion a mini environment that showcases the wares in the booth while creating interest and trust and establishing a brand-personality. No small task, that.

Visual merchandising is meant to connect with customers in a positive manner. To fail to do so means these collectors may look elsewhere, regardless of the quality of the antiques on display. Of course, dealers may have different ideas of what constitutes such a milieu but there are some common elements that should be considered.

One maxim is that design of a store window, display within the store,

The Psychology of a Well-Designed Show Booth

or an antique booth should attract and keep the collector's attention, motivate the customer to enter the booth and look around, stay, and look more, and of course, buy. To accomplish these goals the booth should be visually appealing, a concept that includes color, lighting, use of space, product information, sensory input (touch, smell, sound). The personal interaction between the collector and seller (dealer) is a matter for another time but should not be dismissed or ignored. Color is an especially important element in a booth's ambiance. At higher end shows some dealers play with the color of the booth's walls – black, white, blue, wallpaper, a window with valence, etc. But the major source of color are the objects themselves. Even in booths with brown furniture, paintings, ceramics, and other objects with color should provide interest. Some dealers who sell art have booths awash in color.

I remember as a kid being enthralled by the store windows of Marshall Field's & Co.'s downtown Chicago store windows at Christmas time. Toy trains running, Santa, the sleigh, elves, wrapped presents, snow on the trees, a Christmas tree, star or angel at top, tinsel, bright colors, small town scenes with stores and houses. Even today black and white photos of these displays or seeing such a store window in a movie brings me back to the 50s. While I have never seen a toy train running in a booth at an antique show (wouldn't that be interesting?) I like booths that draw my eye, seduce, whisper to me to look and enter. I know I am looking at a well-designed booth when it bends a finger and invites me to "come hither."

Before Entering a Booth

The view of a booth from the aisle of an antique show is analogous to looking in a department store's window. Its goal should be to attract attention, to highlight what is special, to seduce. Unlike the store windows at Christmastime, this can be difficult to accomplish in a booth crammed to the rafters, the dealer's philosophy seemingly, "The more I bring, the more I have to sell." The problem is that few pieces look special in such an environment (at least to me). It also can be difficult draw and keep a collector's attention if the booth has numerous smalls in rectangular, waist-high display cases. They get in the way. I know –

people would steal smalls if not locked in a case, something fragile will be broken. All no doubt true. Yet my reading and personal experience leads me to believe such display cases must be used judiciously if at all. They simply are off-putting.

Having already waxed nostalgic, let me turn 180 degrees. While the holiday department store window of my youth seemed to almost be crawling with inviting merchandise, a booth less profuse is usually more attractive. A collector who is standing in the aisle can see the treasures within. With a sweep of his eye, he can behold what is for sale. The booth should be well lit, and any cases with smalls should not impede looking or entering. Less is more. The antiques need room and space to speak for themselves and do so loudly and grandly. No items ought to be hidden in dark corners requiring copious effort to be discovered. If a special item sits on a low platform, it should not hide other, equally good antiques. As one dealer told me about designing his booth, "Give the stuff room to breathe."

One element that attracts attention is motion, often seen in the old-time store windows of major department stores at Christmas time – the toy train running or the nodding heads of elves. I have never seen motion used in an antique booth and believe it would be a powerful attraction. Imagine a booth at a high-end show with a wonderful Windsor chair (sitting on a platform for all to see, highlighting the piece) and a drop-front desk on a second platform. Now imagine each platform slowly turning, showing the collector what the chair or desk looks like from all possible angles. The desk's backboards, the view of the chair from the side and rear.

Within the Booth

The more technical term for the layout of a booth once one enters is its "interior display." As already noted, severe and perhaps (to the collector but not necessarily to the dealer) unnecessary clutter and obstacles may frustrate potential buyers. Some dealers are minimalists, with only a few items. Most dealers seem to fall in the middle. Regardless, the interior display should enhance what is for sale, leaving room to view items from multiple viewpoints and to easily walk through the booth.

The Psychology of a Well-Designed Show Booth

And how does a collector walk through a booth? Free form layout allows browsing. In these displays there is no one path in the booth (in contrast to the so-called racetrack display). A collector can walk around an item, approach the booth from more than one direction, turn left or right. This relaxed structure increases sales. I attended one show where a booth of a dealer I visited had three entrances/exits – one to each side and one at the front. Where dealers place items, the platforms on which the items sit, the display cases can create pathways and enhance the display.

Once you enter a booth, a good interior display allows room to look (of course crowds cannot be controlled but hopefully the dealer has not piled items on top of one another so closely that a visitor must sidle if he can move at all). If two or three of the same genres coexist (desks, chairs, tables, Hudson Valley paintings) allow a collector to be able to visually place one next to the other in his mind and compare their virtues.

When it comes to item descriptions and labels, a bit longer account (often "typed" and plastic coated) gives a collector a sense of who, what, where, and when – a mini history lesson if you will. Where was the table made? Who made the weathervane? And if attributed to a certain shop or area, what attributes lead to this conclusion or hypothesis? Many dealers save this "extended" information for verbally presenting to a collector interested in a piece.

As for display cases, interior display with taller, thinner ones with good lighting show off what is within without necessarily interfering with a positive booth design. Personally, the typical display case leaves me flat. I find myself bending over, working hard (too hard?) to see what is within. And items are seldom labeled or described (not enough room I guess). And such display cases seem to break up the ambiance of a booth and physically impede my movement.

The color of a booth's walls, unless flamboyant and off-putting, probably matters less than the design and display that set items off. I think that is why I love to look at booths at high-end shows. The booths seem emptier than their counterparts at many lower-level shows. Fewer items allow those situated within to really "pop."

In summary, the merchandise (antiques) must be visible, easily accessible, and available in a range to choose from. Even in high-end show booths with relatively few objects, a collector typically finds paintings, furniture, ceramics, folk art, and a host of other pieces. The dealer's goal should be to create an emotional connection with the collector who is interested not only in the quality of a piece, but what it will look like in his home. When a dealer's booth and its objects cause a collector to imagine where the object might be placed in his home, and what it would look like there, his imagination has been awakened. When this occurs, there is a better chance the collector will purchase something.

A problem in creating interest is that many dealers' booths are basically the same, show after show. A collector knows who the dealer is whose booth he is looking at regardless of the objects. Such branding by the dealer may communicate "Here I am." It also can be terribly boring. A clichéd booth design can cause collectors to just casually glance at the objects within. The collector knows where the different genres will be displayed. Visual display research argues that the dealer should change the booth's ambiance with some regularity. The same objects may be more appealing and noticeable if they are found in different locations, one show to the next.

Not to be understated, a dealer's booth needs a comfortable place where a sales slip can be written, and the item purchased discussed at more length. Depending on what is being displayed, a couple of chairs and a flat surface (table, chest top) serve the purpose well. The recency effect argues for the power of our most recent memories and communications. A dealer wants the customer going away happy, wanting to return, feeling she has been treated well.

The bottom line is that with a good booth display the dealer could probably sell more antiques at a higher price.

"Well, there you have it," I hear you say. "Those are pretty amorphous concepts – emotional connection, inviting, positive ambiance, attracting attention." Yet I bet you can name a few dealers that always seem to have attractive booths, whether you collect and buy from them or not. Further, I can hear you also say, "Isn't it really easy? (to design an attractive booth), if a dealer has drop-dead gorgeous antique?" Perhaps, but only with good visual display, important to any dealer, even those at the top.

But, we don't quite have it yet. A dealer must seriously consider other variables in trying to design a first-rate booth with all the elements of a powerful and successful visual display.

Let's start with money. A dealer endures costs associated with presenting his goods at an antique show – travel, lodging, show overhead, and then more for display cases, lighting, and his time. If the show is an expensive one the dealer must decide what pieces to bring at what price point. An expensive show requires pieces that sell for more. A less expensive show, with collectors not expecting pieces priced in five or six figures can accommodate lower cost antiques. So, which pieces to bring? And will a lower-level show, with lower-level pieces, allow the dealer to design a booth that pops? Can less expensive antiques pop at all? The answer is yes, depending on how the booth is designed and laid out. A department store can sell a lot of sweaters or other pieces of clothing priced reasonably if the display window outside the store, and the display of sweaters inside the store are creative and beautiful. Antique booths follow the same display rules.

There is another side to money. What is the dealer's experience in how much his booth must be valued at to reach his target revenue for the show? If a booth fee is $2,500 and the dealer wants to make $25,000 what cumulative value of antiques does, he need to bring and display? – $100,000, $150,000? Does he have items that will fit well together in a booth at those price points?

A dealer's booth is also constrained by what he has in inventory. He may well imagine what would increase the attention getting and beauty of his booth but if he does not own those items, he is only dreaming. Of course, he may buy well on the floor before the show opens. Then he is faced with how well and in what ways some of these pieces fit into a booth design – if he does not put them away – that he has worked on for some time.

There also exist issues of dealers' tastes and experiences. Would a pair of nice Philadelphia Chippendale chairs look good next to a gorgeous painted country tavern table? If so in the dealer's opinion, they can be grouped. If the dealer thinks, No, I like to group like with like, he now has two design elements in the booth to juggle, formal and country and may need other pieces to balance both. But space is limited.

The same decisions and juggling are needed regarding smalls, and again, how expensive the smalls are may depend on the show. A couple of beautiful painted small boxes would look out of scale on the top of a high chest of drawers or flat top highboy, and perhaps too busy as well. Does the dealer stack the smalls, and if so, how high a stack? Where to put them to best effect? "On a shelf", I hear you say. Well then, the dealer needs a pewter cupboard or another type of cupboard with shelves, or just a set of shelves. Does he own one? Will it fit in this show and the booth he has in mind? Stay tuned.

And there it finally is: a gorgeous booth. And then the dealer sells well during setup (to other dealers) and the booth's standout star or two are gone. The dealer does not even get a nice photo of his booth in any of the antique publications covering the show. Before the show opens, he must now remake a booth that attracts. And if he sells well on day one of a multi-day show, he must move pieces, add to them, and hope to design an attractive booth for day two and beyond. More than one star for certain locations within the booth are a must.

I never really knew of or thought about many of these issues before working on this chapter. But now that I do, it makes looking at dealers' booth much more interesting. What, I ask myself, is the dealer trying to achieve? Do I find the booth well designed and inviting, both from the aisle and once I enter it? I wonder if there are people who work with dealers to improve their booth design and display (and therefore sales) and if dealers would be open to working with someone with that expertise.

So, the next time you attend an antique show, look at a both from the "meta-perspective." What factors are pulling you in, are leading you to reach for your wallet, are causing you to pause or smile? Who really seems to have mastered visual merchandising? And what do you like in a booth's design? After all is said and done, and I think you will agree with me that selling antiques still comes down to great stuff at a fair price. I'd love to hear from you.

Dealers need to understand, where the eye leads, the heart follows.

Chapter 13

The Realm of Rejected Values and Bad Behavior by Collectors (and Others)

It is comforting to think of those collecting American antiques as a world of virtuous people. The courage and passion inherent in collecting bring a smile to my face. As a former academic I cherish the learning that takes place for any serious collector – of history, what characteristics make a piece an aesthetic delight, obtaining expertise. But these "righteous people" are not and cannot be the sole residents in the world of collecting, more a village if truth be told, in which some inhabitants are no more noble than in any other community.

When Sam died, he found himself not in heaven but the other place. While providing his personal information (hell had a database you wouldn't believe) he listed collecting as one of his hobbies. "You'll be right at home here," one of the devil's assistants informed him. "What did you collect?"

"American antiques," Sam replied.

The devil punched a few keys and looked at his screen. "Ah, apparently you have already been in hell, but we've got a focus group that meets Tuesday nights and another for Friday afternoon. Want me to sign you up?"

So, let's be candid and look at some of the more unfortunate and baser impulses and behaviors, the transgressions, wrong doings, and falls from grace that occur in the village of American antiques. While the damned may not transgress divine law, they surely violate the higher good and our expectations. You surely have seen collectors or dealers be less than upstanding.

Wandering across the borders between the realms of good and evil is hard to avoid, no less so for those who collect antiques. Good intentions regularly fall victim to immediate and practical concerns: cost, profit, the adoration of our peers. The collector's sins represent our immoral and shiftless selves. Why should those of us who revere our past and admire its charms be immune to bad behavior? While these transgressions bear familiar (overly familiar, I fear) names, they express themselves in unique ways when indulged in by the antique collector. I borrow from Dante's Circles of Hell and the Seven Cardinal Sins.

What would we hear at a tent revival of antique collectors, dealers, and the like disclosing their less than righteous behaviors? Plenty, I think. Behold! Clustered around the infernal table was a bevy of hardened sinners, each reluctantly confessing, though clearly not repenting. And this being "the other place," no matter how often those in attendance heard the tales of the damned, it aggravated the living heck out of them on each occasion. And at a side table sat a minor demon, inevitably using a tablet (an iPad to be exact, truly Apple's products were everywhere), taking down the lessons to be learned.

Treachery

Betrayal of trust, using positions of responsibility to one's own ends, cheating, acting dishonestly or unfairly to gain advantage. Encountered the most of any of the sins in the Americana world of sins and nogoodniks. A dealer grossly misrepresenting a piece he knows is not right is a good example.

> James has lied to another dealer about what he received in payment for a piece they both had an interest in. (Yes, a fictional event but I know of several true examples over the years.) Ours is a small world, American antiques, and the cheated dealer has found out. Victoria touches up paint on woodenware and sells it

as in perfect condition. Elizabeth ages furniture by hurrying it along to the desired surface and patina, selling it as original in every way. Mary (none is the queen of England by the way) has a restorer who colludes with her to make pieces look as good as old. William's descriptions of pieces in his shop and at shows always contain the earliest possible date for Circa___, and his histories contain deliberate lies that increase the piece's desirability and price.

Daniel was sending his collection to an auction house to be dispersed. His detailed item descriptions were too honest he decided. He deleted known repairs in the hopes auction personnel and bidders would overlook these faults. To his dismay after auction preview days the word was spread to be careful, many of his pieces were not right. In this case, his deceit was his downfall. Mark was the proud and long-time owner of an auction house that was known for *caveat emptor* (let the buyer beware). While not uncommon to sell items "as is," Mark accepted consignments of pieces he knew were not antiques. In other words, it was not from lack of staff or the time and ability to assess items for genuineness, it was outright fraud (and greedy as well).

Pride

The sin from which all other sins arise. At the heart of pride lies vanity. According to many, we live in the age of narcissism and pride fits comfortably into that universe. The sinner puts her desires, whims, and wants above the welfare of others. To be fully immersed in the sin of pride, you must believe you are essentially better than others, have faith you are without limits and faults, and be blind to others' accomplishments. Witness:

Paula took great pride in her collection, as do many collectors. But her pride was excessive. When other knowledgeable collectors visited – which happened increasingly rarely anymore – to see her latest finds, Paula always knew best. Other collectors could not point her to dealers she might consider working with, breach the question of upgrades (nothing in her collection needed upgrading according to Paula), and whatever they owned could not compare to her treasures. "Junk," she was heard to mutter. And Paula wouldn't help other collectors any which way.

Unhappily, the Paulas of collecting exist. Something about a little knowledge lights a fuse in some people, tickles their sense of specialness and renders them overbearing. Though we have all been told "pride cometh before the fall," the veracity of that adage must work itself out in a fallen world of lost values and lost friends.

Gluttony

An inordinate desire to consume more than one needs.

Andy was insatiable. He was not a binge eater, he was a binge collector. All of that might have been well and good, but he did not treat other collectors ("the enemy," he called them) well. When he had to have a piece, which was often, he would cut others' hearts out to get it. How many candlestands or firkins does one need? Well, if you knew Andy the answer was "more." Not a hoarder – many pieces in his collection were quite good – he stuffed antiques into his house the way someone who overeats pushes food into his mouth. A combination of gluttony and anger made Andy a lonely collector.

Lust

Inordinate craving for the body's pleasures. Not merely a strong craving, lust is an insatiable want. We can lust after others but also things.

Rick had abandoned his wife psychologically. No, not for another woman – that she could have understood – but for antiques. He lusted after them. As one would expect, his lust took the form of obsessing about, dreaming of, fantasizing about and craving antiques. Finding a great addition to his collection lessened his lust not one iota. It was objects he craved, wanted to caress, had to look at. When he talked with other collectors, he made their passions for antiques seem like mere infatuations, likings, not loving. He had abandoned his marriage, family, and friends to his lust.

Sloth

Avoidance of spiritual or physical work. Some writers and observers of current society argue, quite persuasively I might add, that many of us need more sloth in our lives. We are busy, too busy, disconnected from our inner selves, from others, from nature - in essence from our lives. We are so busy living our lives that we cannot slow down and process and make sense of them.

Scott was a slothful collector. He was passive, idle, and made little effort. He expected dealers to come to him with their latest finds. When he went to a show – now. that took effort on his part – he was always resentful to hear about what had sold and was no longer available. That's what happens when you get to a show several hours after it has opened. As part of passivity, he didn't keep up on the market: what was available or rarely seen, or about what items were selling for. He struggled to build the collection he wanted but it was no wonder he did so. He often was cheated, overpaid, bought items of lesser quality. But because he struggled, he demeaned others, spread vicious gossip about dealers and fellow collectors (notice the anger present here as well).

Anger

Occurs in someone who rejects love and chooses fury instead. Best thought of as wrath. Typically anger occurs when we feel unrecognized as a person or think of ourselves as the object of unfairness.

Mitch went through his collecting life angry. If an auctioneer failed to recognize his bid in a timely manner (read nanosecond) Mitch seethed. He was angry if a dealer sold something he liked to someone else, if a show did not open precisely at the publicized time, if a dealer did not pay attention to him the instant that he entered a booth. Mitch had never known the meaning of "easy going, live and let live, or fair is what happens." Being angry might well have just raised his blood pressure but Mitch made it his practice to let the world know of the injustices that he had undergone. He fumed, vented, raised his voice, confronted others (he did not discriminate – other collectors, dealers, show promoters, auction house staff). He was known by those in the antique world as "resentful Mitch." He was even angry about how isolated he was, although it was clear to everyone but him that his behaviors pushed others away.

Envy

Coveting what someone else has or resenting their success or good fortune in life. A base for unhappiness, murder (Cain murdered Abel because he believed Abel was more favored by God). No good comes from envy, as an envious person often wishes or brings misfortune to others.

Edward, or Eddie the Envious (sounds like the name of a British monarch) was not satisfied with his collection, even though it was quite nice. Measuring himself by what he owned, he had never learned that it is the journey that makes life meaningful and may lead to happiness or satisfaction, not reaching one's goals. Eddie's deepest wish was to be recognized as having one of the best collections of Americana ever put together. That was a rarified ambition to say the least, and Eddie was hypersensitive to never quite achieving it. Of course, collectors existed with more financial means, better luck, a keener eye. Eddie was envious of them all. He dreamed of some of these collectors getting divorced or dying an untimely death so their collections would reenter the market, and he talked about such ungenerous thoughts with others. Constantly bemoaning his lot in life, Eddie begrudged anyone, who for whatever reason (hard work, diligent preparation, etc.) found pieces that <u>should</u> have been his.

Greed

Ignoring the world of the spiritual, one desires material wealth or gain. Avarice comes to mind.

You would expect to find greed in the antique market, as one does in all markets, and you would not be disappointed. But sometimes irony is beautiful. Mike was a collector who always was on the edge of larceny. He delayed paying what he owed, hoping to wear the dealer down or so exasperate him that he'd get a better deal. But the dealer he was trying to leverage had sold him a weathervane that wasn't what it was represented as. Cheaper to omit a couple of repairs and to represent the piece as original when the surface, beautifully enhanced I might say, was not original at all. So, there we have the two crooks, if I may so bold, locked in combat, each using every trick at their disposal to cheat the other. The dealer had the advantage over Mike. It didn't matter to him if Mike wore him down some. The vane, not being the genuine article, was not worth one-tenth of what Mike had agreed to pay for it. Counterbalanced levels of greed made for a marriage made in heaven, though Mike and the dealer probably ended down under.

Sadly, I am convinced my list of sins and examples may well be the tip of a transgression iceberg. If you are concerned that someday you'll be signing up for one of those diabolical focus groups, there is still time to mend your ways. Not to be cynical, but the American antique world of collecting is a marketplace, and wouldn't we expect items to be misrepresented in one way or another if there is profit to be made? I would. But let's not place greed and other unseemly behavior only at the doorstep of dealers or auction houses. We collectors bear a responsibility also to be virtuous or attempt to be so.

There you have it. To collectors of Americana the "shining city on a hill" is how they would like the American antique world to be. But, alas, sometimes it is not. May your journey to that shining city be one of exemplary behavior. Or someone might be saying to you, "See you at our next Friday group meeting."

Ethics and rules of conduct exist for all residents in a community, including the village of American antiques.

Section III

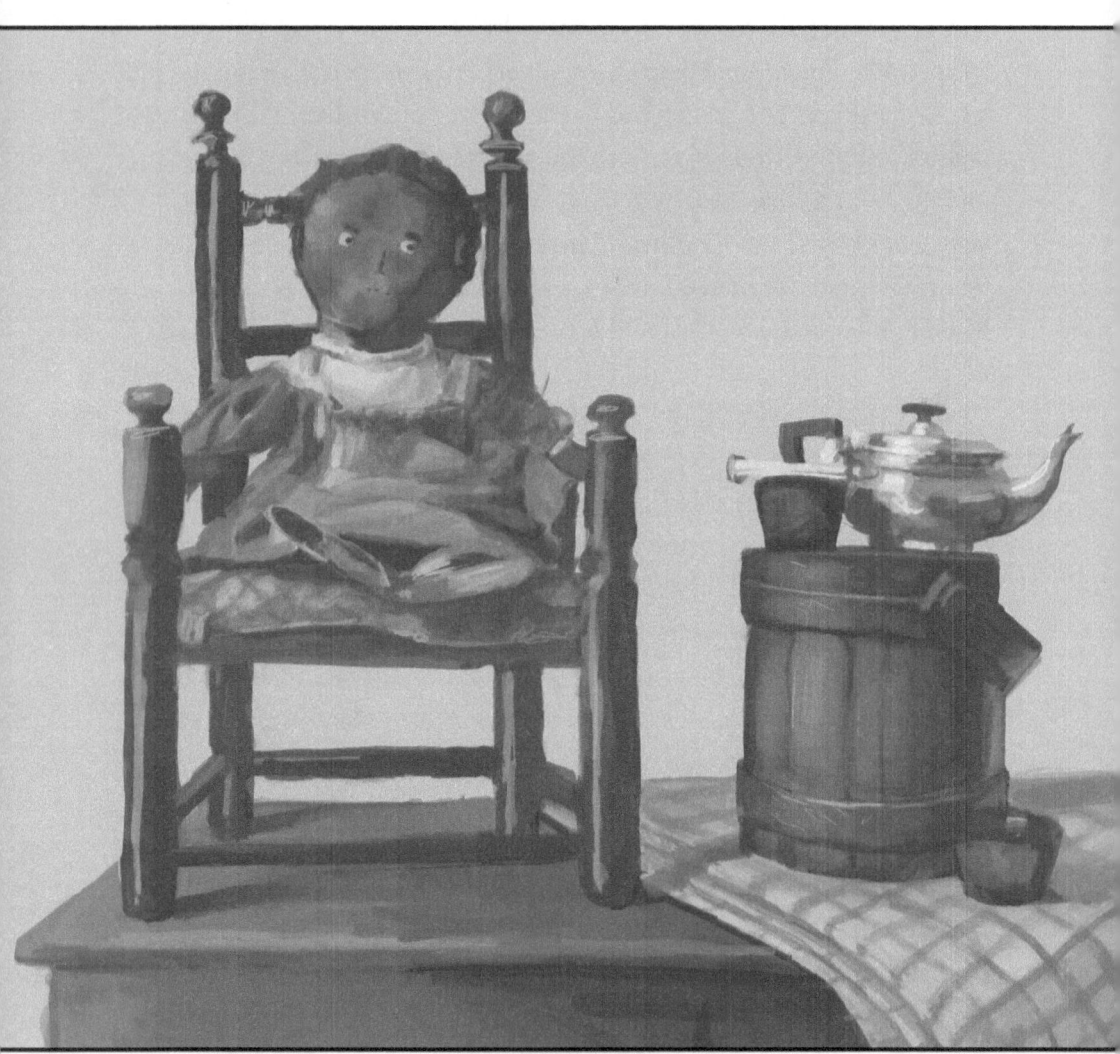

Self Reflection
Isn't Just For Self

Chapter 14
American Antiques are a Window to Our Nation's Past, Present and Future

As an avid collector of American antiques, I admit to being guilty of sometimes taking history for granted, even ignoring it. I should pause more often to wonder about what my antiques say about America, whose hands wore their surfaces and paint, and how they managed to survive. The true significance of the hard-won treasures we own, keeping our nation's narrative alive, too often seems little but background noise to "freshness," provenance, rarity and aesthetics. I should hold in awe a table crafted before the American colonies formed a nation. I should revere a Bachelder map of the Battle of Gettysburg – the conflict part of our country's soul – still drawing attention and analyses 150 years after the last cannon fired.

Our antiques' histories give them their meaning and even additional value. That pewter mug is nothing but an old container, at least until we know why pewter was so popular once upon a time, who made it, who owned it, why it was cherished as a family heirloom. The history of a piece, frankly, may be more important than the antique itself. George Santayana's most famous quote bears repeating: "Those who cannot remember the past are condemned to repeat it." Without history we are set adrift, making up our values and goals as we go.

Self-Reflection Isn't Just for Self

History provides much of our nation's identity (and loyalty). Take as an example the bald eagle. Here it stands, carved from wood, forged as a weathervane, inlaid in a piece of furniture - the symbol of our nation's strength and high ideals (a good thing Franklin failed in his effort to have the turkey acknowledged as America's symbolic bird).

Or consider the flag in its many variations, each speaking for an era of progress or conflict or failure (specifically, the Stars and Bars, that retains so many elements of what we have come to think of as Old Glory). Our flag both calls forth and symbolizes patriotism and American values, wars fought, won . . . and more recently lost. That lowly table sat in bygone taverns and tells its tale of lodging, meeting, dining, drinking, gossip, gambling and gamboling.

My point is simple. We bear a responsibility to use the antiques we collect to advocate, promote, educate about, advance, and champion our nation's history. Collectors need to move beyond "the look" and value scholarship of our collections' histories. In truth, an antique is a mute witness waiting to narrate the wonder of our nation's past, guiding us to understand its present. It begs for someone – and who better than a knowledgeable collector? – to lend it a voice.

What lies in an antique is part and parcel of our nation's story, its aspirations, its accomplishments, and its disappointments. Like the stage manager in the play *Our Town*, the antique introduces us to a vanished and ill-remembered cast of characters, teaching us about an America gone by. Unlike the stage manager, the antique invites us not only to watch, but also to take part in the past. It makes history come alive. It lets us momentarily be involved the Revolutionary War, our industrial beginnings, the fight over slavery.

An antique is more than just a thing. In its moment it embraced our nation's loftiest philosophers, called forth the skills of masters and journeymen of lost arts, or challenged the ideas, tastes and aspirations of people much like us.

Were I to pen such a tale it would be a first-person account of a simple firkin or tavern table, documenting the kitchens or rooms in which "I" sat and what "I" heard and observed throughout the decades, how the average person lived and to what he aspired. Yes, firkin or table as raconteur.

Huzzah to the dealer who described a child's Chippendale chest as an "eye-witness to American revolution history." That little treasure, probably Connecticut in origin, set me wondering who, amidst the tumultuous times of revolt and partisanship, serenely had a chest crafted for his child. While some were more affected by the revolution than others, craftsmen continued to make furniture, and life went on. Amid the hoorah of popular history, with crackling guns and pounding drums, a child was being gifted with a miniature that would be cherished . . . and survive right down to our own, (to some) troubled times. Imaginatively, that one little antique offers the thoughtful one heck of an education regarding the realities of the American War of Independence, the inevitability of treasuring that which brings pleasure, and the random forces behind sheer survival. It can teach about the truth that Homefront life always "goes on," regardless of the war being waged.

A single object, in this case a chest of drawers, can open the door to philosophy, economics, law, exhortations, the nation's expansion, hopes and fears, war and peace, its citizens' yearnings, ways of life, transportation, and geography. Our beloved antiques offer an insight into the mundane and extraordinary, into great ideas and material culture – how those who came before us lived every day, what our society and its citizens read, valued, and heeded, a reflection of both the high (think famous painters and their paintings, sculptors and their statues) and the low (wooden bowls, kitchen objects, everyday furniture, and yes, a firkin or tavern table).

Our narrative starts with the object's name, when and where it was made, its purpose if not evident, and the materials used in crafting it. If a collector emphasizes technology, we might learn the about the craft techniques used in its construction, how long it took to make the object, and if the object was made by hand when it transitioned to being machine made (if ever). And what powered those machines – water, steam, electricity?

We must remember the training (apprenticeship, etc.) the craftsman possessed and what such an education entailed. Or the formally trained artist as compared with an itinerant limner. Was the craftsman expert in more than one specialty (woodwork, ironwork)? What do we know about these craftsmen – their socio-economic makeup, gender, how hard a life they lived, and whether the American dream was alive in the 18th and 19th centuries, and how if that dream has changed today? What do the answers to those questions say about the history of our nation?

To learn about an evolving and growing nation and its transportation, a collector's essay/story/knowledge of a single piece in his collection could roam widely – where the object was made, the size of the village or hamlet, or nature of the area (Connecticut River Valley, Lehigh Valley, Philadelphia). Was this area a center of such objects (e.g., clocks, blanket chests, redware plates, formal furniture)? How did one travel to and from this area (water, wagon, horseback, train)?

To study consumer wants and needs, fads, and eras, did an object have ornamentation and if so, why? What made the decorative element necessary or popular? When was the object followed by something in a different material or style that became a new trend?

If we are to learn about economics, what was the object's cost and its selling price? Was that expensive for the era in which it was made? How did its purchaser earn the money to buy it? Was barter used? Who was likely to purchase the object (someone wealthy, for example)?

Collectors can take antiques in hand and journey through the nation's past to the present, leapfrogging from one theme to another – transportation, war and peace, changing lifestyles, the nation's boundaries and expansion, and patriotism.

Using American antiques to bring our nation's history to life and at the same time educating, seems a task for which we collectors are well suited. Failing to do so is how we are currently shortchanging ourselves and contributing to history's fade into the background. We need more amazement at the lives the objects we collect have lived. And we need to share that awe with others.

American antiques make history come alive and educate on the nation's present and future.

Chapter 15

Collectors' Angst: What will We Do With Our Collections?

"To every thing there is a season, and a time for every purpose under heaven:"

Ecclesiastes 3:1, King James Version

When in Manchester, New Hampshire for antiques' week a while ago I talked with lots of collectors awaiting shows' openings. In my informal discussions, one theme repeatedly emerged. Beloved objects that make up collections have become or are becoming a burden. As I looked at those waiting for The Collectors' Fair to open, for example, I opined that the median age of the group was 75 (i.e., half were older and half younger). Though they clearly had not lost their passion for collecting, the question of how to dispense with what they had so painstakingly assembled was of more than passing concern. The issue for these collectors, all getting on in years, as they whisper to each other and would have shouted to the rooftops if they could: "What will I do with my collection?"

Such angst may also have a psychological basis. Objects can have great meaning to us and parting with them oftentimes entails very real loss, grief, and nostalgia for happier bygone times. Aging collectors may also find that pondering what to do with beloved antiques vivifies their feelings of mortality and confronts them with end-of-life (or nearing-end-of-life) issues with which that they may be uncomfortable.

Those with whom I spoke had accepted the fact that nothing, not collecting and not ourselves, is forever. Their angst stemmed from the difficulties of finding a clearly marked pathway to their collections' dispersals. What feasible alternatives had these folks considered?

Not one had seen the path of doing nothing and letting their heirs simply divvy the hoard. Solutions seems to be two-pronged. First, liquidating as much of the collection as they could while they were still alive. As you will see, while this solution is practical, the question of exactly how one is to disperse a collection is tricky. Add to that the fact that it takes courage to calmly say goodbye to a treasured part of one's life and to treasured objects. Second, they recognized the need to prepare to have the collection dispersed by a trusted family member, friend, or executor.

In preparation, collectors with whom I spoke had drafted detailed lists of pieces they owned and had talked with their estate's executor, typically one of their children, about where to find this information. Because it only seems prudent, I too have such a list describing each piece in my wife and my collection, the cost when purchased, photographs, who it was purchased from, and so forth. But even a minutely detailed list is insufficient when it comes to assessing values, and most of these collectors have named a person or source their executor was to contact when the time came. The problem, and you may already have encountered it, is that many (most?) of the dealers from whom we have bought our treasures are aging right along with us and may not still be in the business when we or our representatives want to deacquisition our precious pieces. And of course, these persons who say they will auction or help us sell what is dear to us may change their mind sometime in the future. Even in the present, they can only broker so many antiques. I talked with one well-known dealer (I will not identify the genre he specializes in to provide anonymity) who told me that he was getting three to five calls or emails a week asking him to broker a piece for a collector, or worse value a whole oeuvre. In almost all cases he had to decline. The pieces were not special enough or the demand insufficient to allow him to move them a timely manner and make some dollars doing so.

Even in a perfect world where there are dealers who specialize in a particular genre we collect, problems still exist. Whom can we trust? With whom would be comfortable brokering or selling our treasures? And, of course, not everyone has children to step in their stead (I will not mention the word <u>trust</u> here again, though I might). What is a collector to do? A few of them, aware of their dilemma, had found no solution. Several collectors had left instructions for executors about which auction house to have sell their pieces. Again, will these auctions houses be in business in the future, will they still be known and specialize for what they are now, and still have the positive reputation they might today? The answers are unknown.

Collectors can enlist the help of family, friends, fellow collectors and dealers with necessary decisions. Nonetheless, such planning, as I have mentioned, can be difficult. The collection my wife and I have amassed like many, I imagine, requires more than one auction house. – one for Americana, another for my wife's airplane posters, a third for her toy airplane collection, a fourth . . . (As an aside, even though I have designated an auction house to my executor and have contacted it about how to proceed, I do not know if I would have the courage to attend the auction of my pieces if I were physically able to do so.)

Another issue arose related to auction houses. Almost to a person those with whom I talked shook their heads at the cost and perceived complexities of having their collections sold at auction. They knew it was a process with many details to be worked through, an action fraught with potential problems. Yet, they also knew that auction houses need to make a profit and dispensing of antiques via one is no more difficult (although still tricky) than many other such undertakings they had faced.

One solution collectors touched upon that seemed to provide much solace was to auction or otherwise deaccession their collections, but keep several favorite pieces. Knowing which few objects to keep or give to others may not be as daunting as originally assumed. I know which pieces I would want to surround me. And I would hire a professional photographer to take close ups of favorite pieces and then blow up and frame just a part of many, hanging a mélange of "fragments" on my wall.

I do not mean to imply that collectors of antiques have it any more difficult as they age than others. Shakespeare's King Lear makes it clear they do not. But it is disheartening to listen to ardent collectors who love Americana and enjoy passionate collecting struggling with discouraging, if realistic issues, especially at a time when historical awareness is in less repute than it once was in our society and the number of young collectors is dwindling.

Collectors do attempt to sell their pieces themselves. Some use eBay, others sell directly with no on-line platform. I do not know what successes they enjoy. An on-line forum (listserv developed by a collector, dealer or dealer association, auction house, or publication) in which collectors could ask questions and share problems about divesting their collection or upgrading and selling pieces would be useful. Perhaps that same platform could broker items for sale.

One collector had what I thought was an ingenious idea. Would it be possible, he wondered, to have an annual "show" where it was collectors (or others) who had small booths selling items from their collections to other collectors and dealers? Intriguing, I thought. Of course, there were mobility issues lurking. Collectors from the Midwest such as myself or our executors might struggle to bring items to New England, the logical location for such a fair, but I thought the idea had merit. Could it be done on-line? Alternatively, aging collectors might collectively hire a trustworthy manager and set up their own group shop selling their collections, with instructions on what and where items are to be auctioned if they do not sell in a defined time period. There already are people who help us to decide what to take and not take when we leave our homes and go to managed in-home care or health care. Plenty of financial, social, and family counseling is already out there, offered by experts. We need such persons for antiques.

Fascinatingly, few with whom I talked mentioned leaving specific objects to heirs in their wills, mostly because of the grantees' perceived lack of interest. Such a decision requires careful consideration. Yes, we read and know that our children are not interested in our antiques but

What Will We Do With Our Collections?

there still may be an object or two with special meaning they may want desperately and, more importantly, we want them to have. The piece need not be pricey. What is paramount is its meaning to you or to the son or daughter, friend or institution that makes you want to pass it on – its story, aura, or deeper meaning. If you have such objects, you probably want to write out a few lines as why it is so special, that you hope whom you leave it to will enjoy it as much as you did and think of your collecting and you as they do.

Another alternative is to pass your ideas and values that communicate who you are to your heirs and executor, and let them use this document as the basis for dispersing (or holding on to) your collection. Such a document has no legal standing but is called an "ethical will" and has existed in Jewish cultures for a very long time. For example, my ethical will would state that I would not want items donated to a museum if they are to disappear into an archive never to be seen again. I would rather have them shown at a local museum if it was interested and then sold. I would want my pieces to go to good homes but how one assures that is beyond me. I would love to have some of the pieces go to young collectors. And I have thought of having a percentage of the proceeds from my collection, once sold and gone, go to a specific charity or two. You get the idea (and I would love to hear yours).

The uncertainties of collectors regarding dispersing their treasures was not paralyzing or dispiriting. They waited patiently in line, aching once again to fall in love with just one more piece to take home and add to their collections. I know I did, and was disappointed when I found an item I really loved but my wife did not. But I was heartened by the fact I can still have and cuddle that feeling of oh my, that is absolutely wonderful. (Another aside, the only reason I had the opportunity to purchase the piece – wisely denied – was because I was near the front of the New Hampshire Dealers' Association show line. I guess I will be in line early for the rest of my collecting life. This time it would have paid off handsomely, if only I had defied my spouse's wishes.)

I keep returning to the idea of an "antique advisor." similar to a financial advisor. I am only aware of one or two folks who identify themselves as such, and they are older than I am. The process could be straightforward. Most of us already pay a standardized fee for financial advice, and the expert would follow that practice. After providing an inspection and talking to the collector, he would produce a report, listing the items in the collection likely to be sold and suggest vendors who might auction individual holdings off. Naturally, this report would be updated on a regular basis. In effect, we would be ready no matter what happened. It could even be agreed the expert would facilitate to collections dispersal for an hourly of set fee.

I remember visiting my parents' condo after my mother, who had been a widow for a few years, had decided it was time to move to a stepped community. She was dismayed her treasured pots and pans found no home in her children's kitchens. They were expensive once upon a time, after all, and she had touched and used them for many years. Those who collect Americana, like my mother's kitchenware, want them passed along. They are worth something, less financially than in what they say about our lives. Yes, collectors want an equitable return on what their collections are worth monetarily, but I believe that it is our needs for preserving history continuity, identity, and how we lived our lives that is embodied in our collections. The desire to be remembered after one's passing is a natural one, to be in someone's memory, even if only for a generation or two. Our antiques, so important to us, are one way, perhaps, of doing so. The problem is how to go about it all.

And thus, we return to where we began, how to disperse of our collections. Such decisions are but one life event out of many older collectors face. Depending on the health of dear friends, spouse, or children, there are worse things in the world than having lived a full life "antiquing." To everything there is a season, a time for every purpose. For many collectors, age it is the season of preparation and forethought.

As a wise man once said, "What we leave of ourselves becomes our selves." Our treasures have a life of their own.

Chapter 16

The Frenzy for Fresh to the Market

"Fresh to the market" antiques seem as desirable to collectors as fresh to the market corn on the cob, tomatoes or other vegetables at a farmer's stand. Dealers talk up pieces in their shops and show booths as untouched by the eyes of collectors. Entire shows take pride in antiques that have not been shopped around. Auction houses get in the act – all of which got me thinking about the psychology behind the frenzy for freshness.

What exactly does fresh-to-the-market mean? I cannot find an agreed-upon definition. An antique dealer I know had a piece for sale that had been offered to buyers five or six years ago (not by him and at a higher price). It did not sell then. This dealer did not necessarily consider it fresh. Folks knew of its existence, knew what its price was a few years ago, and so forth. But it had been out of sight. Still to many fellow collectors with whom I have talked fresh seems to be: A piece not on a dealer's website for any length of time, an antique they were excited to see, something not recently sold at auction, an antique they were not aware of. It was "fresh" if it had been at auction far enough in the past to make the antique's reappearance on the market special.

All of which begs the question: Is something back on the market after being out of sight for ten years or twenty years resurrected and therefore "fresh"? I have no answer for how long a piece must reside in a collection to be considered new and captivating when it is for sale again.

Self-Reflection Isn't Just for Self

Perhaps mimicking the Supreme Court's Justice Potter Stewart's famous quote (talking about pornography and what is obscene), "I know it when I see it," collectors know what is and is not fresh to the market when they see it. Again, and as always, the social scientist in me wants to survey collectors, dealers and auctioneers to gather data on what this oft-used term really means. Another time.

Fresh to the market can be a positive trait, something to be valued. Many serious collectors know a good deal about what is available within the genres they collect and covet prime pieces new to the show floor or fresh at auction. They may have holes in their collections or want to upgrade less desirable pieces they already possess. Nothing currently on the market, as best as they are aware, fills their needs. Waiting in line at a show where some/many pieces are "fresh" (by their subjective definition) means there may be a few exemplars that are not only fresh but also "good," items that are rare or in wonderful condition. Perhaps the antique came from the hand of a craftsman who is widely known and whose pieces seldom enter the marketplace, or the example is an exceptional one, or it evinces a form unusual for the maker. In such cases, fresh earns its plaudits. Some collectors purchase entire collections, think stacks of boxes or firkins, for example. If such a collection is not available, perhaps one will be on the show floor today – fresh.

When I wrote about why collectors collect (*Come Collect with Me*, 2019) one of the powerful and central motivators were the stories that accompanied items they purchased. Items fresh to the market often have wonderful stories attached to them, stories that a collector has not heard before, that make them irresistible (including the answer to the mysterious question, "Where have you been all these years?"). The particular piece may be no better than others that have been for sale for some time, yet its story is fresh and appealing, making the piece undeniably attractive.

Another reason collectors collect is competitiveness. Beating someone to getting a piece you really like feels good (I was going to write "to some collectors" but felt a sweeping statement was more honest). If someone else wants the antique and I manage to obtain it, good for me. For items fresh to the market that are bought in the first hour or two of

The Frenzy for Fresh to the Market

a show or after being listed on a website, a collector may find the piece special because he bought it before someone else could. It is in his collection. It validates him as a collector.

Obviously, (although I believe it is not obvious at all) pieces fresh to the market are not necessarily good or meet our criteria for aesthetics, style, and connoisseurship. But you wouldn't know that, oftentimes. This truth does not seem talked about much, or if it is, it is discussed in low voices, whispers and murmurs. Many pieces fresh to the market are equal in quality – and sometimes not even as good – as items known to be for sale. Why then does "fresh" carry with it such ringing approbation?

One reason is conformity. Conformity is a term regularly found in the writings of social psychologists. Going with the flow (to put it another way) is omnipresent, the most common form of complying with social values. As humans, we are powerfully motivated to follow the crowd, even though such lackeying has a negative connotation. Yet if all the ships entering a bay use only one access (a haven where you have been told two entrances have sufficient keel depth), wouldn't you be better off to follow in these ships' wakes? Conformity does not mean one has lost one's free will or ability to think critically.

Hence, too, if the collecting world most or all of the time talks about being fresh to the market and thinks it to be "good," collectors may casually assume the trope is the truth. They conform. I conform. And we eagerly look forward to seeing fresh merchandise. At least it's a soothing thought.

Another reason antiques fresh to the market may be considered desirable is because of a psychological phenomenon I have written about previously: habituation. For positive, practical, even defensible genetic reasons, we humans fail to notice (see, smell, hear) stimuli to which we are repeatedly exposed. You do not want every blade of waving grass to be a novel sight, consuming your attention day after day. You want to notice the wild animal crouched in it waiting to dine on you. Anyone who has tried to sell his or her home in a difficult market knows of habituation. Yes, the home may not have sold because the price was too high, or because the owner refused to spend sufficiently on items that enhanced its curb appeal, or it needed a nicer kitchen, a new roof, and storm windows.

Self-Reflection Isn't Just for Self

That is when the real estate broker may suggest pulling the shack off the market for a while. "Let's put it back on the market next spring," says she, "when it can be fresh again." Take away the habituation and suddenly you have a (ahem!) "new" manse for sale.

How narrowly do collectors look at items that have appeared in dealers' booth or on their websites time after time? I would guess not closely at all. At shows, we are accustomed to seeing that rooster weathervane, that table from some undefined moment in the early 19th century, that (yawn!) work of art. We have seen them all before, probably more than once, looked at them and condemned them to the "found wanting" category. If you could erase a collector's memory, and he saw the same piece for the first time at a show that is known for offering new finds, I wonder what his response would be? Most likely positive.

There also exists a powerful cognitive reason why we may disregard items that have lingered on the market for some time. It passes as something rational, though it is far from it. There is a syllogism many collectors use: "Items that have been on the market for a long time have been found wanting by my fellow collectors. This piece has lingered on the market for a long time. Therefore, there is something wrong with it." One of the things that drives dealers crazy is having an antique that is perfect in every way that for one reason or another has failed to sell, time after time. By then collectors are convinced it has been vetted and is flawed, even when in fact there is nothing wrong with it at all.

I once had a dealer tell me that he could put together a wonderful antique collection of items purchased late on the last day of antique shows, or that had sat ignored on dealers' websites or in their shops or booths for more than six months. I did not challenge him, for I believe he is correct. I think that the shaky notion that if something has not sold over time it is therefore flawed, and that engrained cliché simply overpowers a collector's judgment and nerve. More collector courage is needed.

There is a lot to learn from the real estate business if you want to be a collector. One lesson is this: The emotional effect of buying a costly asset often causes buyers to want other people to endorse its value because their "knowledge" validates the buyer's decision. In this day of instant Internet access, new listings (even those that are new only because they

The Frenzy for Fresh to the Market

are re-introduced after an absence) are always at the top of the customer's search. Remember fresh equals good. The realtor says, "The home could go fast. It may already have an offer. It must be seen." I believe the sense of emotional well-being inspired by others' validation helps explain the draw freshness exercises in the antique world.

From another perspective if you believe the fresh to the market chair you purchased is better than ones on the market for some time, you will feel rewarded. Most of the time there is no downside to buying a fresh item, unless you are unforgivably foolish. But buy an antique that has been for sale for a long time, simply because of the courage of your convictions, and you may face a gauntlet of comments. "You bought that?" "I've seen that for months. Why in the heck did you buy it?" "Oh my." And so forth. I once had a dealer tell me of a painting that had been for sale for over two years. Within 24 hours he had not one but two inquiries, both from potential buyers who believed in it. They had no hesitation in defending their purchase. As a matter of fact, they were proud of their taste and loved the painting. Sometimes collectors need strength.

I want to shift gears now and enter the realm of fresh to the market from a somewhat different angle. I have had dealers recount a phenomenon I have trouble understanding: collectors, who when they purchase an item at an antique show, ask that the antique be immediately removed from sight (hidden away, taken off the floor). The same request is made for some pieces purchased from websites. The collector asks that the photo and description be removed, even if the piece been displayed and described for some time – even though no one knows who bought the antique.

It is as if hiding the piece from view makes it more special, lowers its exposure, and keeps it fresh – in the collector's opinion, mind you. I have never heard a reasonable explanation for such behavior. To me it sounds like a delusion. A delusion is a false belief that the item is more special because it is out of sight, despite rational arguments to the contrary. Does taking something off the market somehow make it better because the clock has started ticking on the number of years it will be before it is seen or offered again? I guess in some collectors' minds it does. Would such a collector be more likely to purchase a piece a dealer is brokering as not yet really "on the market" instead of at auction? Probably. An auction house, in order to fulfill obligations to the consignor, must market items to the widest possible audience and often makes them known to collectors most likely to be interested in and to bid on the antique. One could argue the fresh quickly becomes "unfresh."

Could it be the behavior has nothing to do with freshness at all, that there are two types of collectors, those who love to share their collections and those who enjoy them exclusively? The latter might tell you "I have it and no one else can see it" or "I am the only one who can let you see it," thereby gaining power and control. I am speculating, obviously. Such antique aficionados might remove a piece from view if that form of power or control were important to them.

So, there you have it. The frenzy for freshness may be simple and suitable at your farmer's market. But in the antique world it may be, but perhaps not. A piece fresh to the market could be just what a collector has been seeking. On the other hand, as someone told me, fresh is "a fallacy whispered, sometimes shouted, hoping to find the ear of an easy victim." As I have written many times, collecting is a human endeavor and we collectors are complicated indeed. That is one reason why collecting is such fun.

Fresh-to-the-market is more of a magical charm than a criterion.

Chapter 17

Mine

You have just handed a dealer a check at a prestigious antique show. "The antique is mine," you say to yourself. A curator and a researcher at a museum have just taken ownership of a wonderful Philadelphia chair. "The chair is ours," they say. The word <u>mine</u> could not be clearer. But what exactly does ownership and something being "mine" mean?

Believe it or not there are overbearing rules for ownership, legal and social. The fact you want something to be yours or believe something is yours is fraught with uncertainty and sometimes drama. The antiques we own help define who we are. They are part of our being. At the same time, they are part of a larger community or communities, *n'est pas*? Perhaps you figuratively "stole" the antique you just purchased at the show, or a dealer "stole" it from you when he made an offer on it in your home. You stole the precious piece because the dealer did not know what he had, though you did, and vice versa. Is the purchase fair, right or legal? Does it affect how you think about what is yours?

Can you blithely destroy rare, historically significant antiques because they are yours without consequences? Was the Saudi Mohammed bin Salman justified in keeping his Michelangelo out of the Louvre out of spite? He paid hundreds of millions for <u>Salvator Mundi</u>. If he wants to keep it hidden from the public, shouldn't he be able to? Can he deface, disburse, destroy it?

Self-Reflection Isn't Just for Self

Perhaps what is mine is not mine alone?

A perfect example of "mine" is a family heirloom, a piece you have admired for some time that a sibling or other relative also covets. If so, you truly are a caretaker rather than an owner, weighed down by family history, knowing that – barring exceptional and unforeseen circumstances – the antique will not be sold but passed along to the next generation. In my family that object is a samovar that my father's parents brought from Russia when they emigrated. How they transported it across the sea and kept it safe is beyond me.

If, instead, multiple family members lust for the same item, any good vibrations you experience about the antique being yours may be dulled by ill will and soured with acrimony. "Mine" is not always a sweet melody. Frequently its lyric is that of alienation. Yes, the piece is yours, but when possessive feelings intervene, it may bear an emotional price far higher than what your antique might cost in dollars on the open market.

You can read about such a rocking chair with no dollar value, I might add, in the book *Mine*, when one heir simply took it and a second heir contested his ownership in court. The deceased's will was silent on who should have the piece, creating the ownership dilemma. The lack was understandable. It was only a simple chair, although the emotional attachments of the parties rendered it anything but simple or valueless. The case judge's alternatives would have taxed Solomon's wisdom: Saw it in half, assign joint chair custody, give it to the heir who took it (first come first served), give it to the other heir (first to the courthouse), auction it off and let the heir with the most money (or most nerve) buy it, flip a coin, deny it to either, let the judge let the matter undecided until the two can agree, burn the danged thing. The judge's final decision: six months each year at each of the disputants' residence. It is not clear who had to schlep it to and fro. So, the chair was "mine" for each, six months of the year.

Pieces in your collection, "mines" if you will, are not simply grabbed or plucked from a dealer, auction house, or another collection. They require resources to acquire, but more importantly knowledge, preparation, luck (that in many cases you made), and serendipity. Thus, the stories that accompany many of our prized possessions. Mines are the result of toil and the sweat of our collecting labors, a fact that noncollectors fail to fully appreciate, at least as we see it. Furthermore, pieces in our collections may cause others disappointment and anguish. We seldom think about the losing bidders when we are successful at an auction, the person just behind us at a show looking at and reaching for the antique we just told the dealer we would take. Ignore the fact that we, personally, may have had a similarly disappointing experience or two in the past. Mines seem to involve what's good for the goose is good for the gander, as we all lose out now and then. Despite the fact, empathy is rare.

We collectors spend a lot of time on the issue of what's mine. If I like or love an American antique, I want it to be mine. As I look at its gorgeous photograph online, touch it at an auction preview or in a dealer's booth or shop, the feeling is intensified. I can fantasize that will be mine. At a show if I see it first and put a verbal hold on it, it is mine (usually). If you are looking at a piece at a show and put it down, it may become mine. And then there's the dealer rule: If you break it, it is yours. Instant possession. And a lousy way to get a crippled mine.

And when a dealer is willing to let you purchase one of his mines, it takes on a special cachet. Somehow an antique is special when a dealer tells us it has been in his collection, sat in his living room, been used in his home for years and he is now putting it on the market. His mine can become yours. The same feeling of desirability exists for a mine that has been off the market for some time. Possession by someone allegedly tasteful, rarity, even the envy of others (dare I again mention MBS's Michelangelo?) is a sort of secular baptism, endorsing and validating the desirability – hence worth – of an antique.

We all know that the issue of possession is a duchy in the legal realm. The rocking chair story is a good example. Thus, the oftentimes long columns in *Maine Antique Digest* and other publications about lawsuits, countersuits, court rulings, items pulled from auction, federal law on what cannot be sold, broken promises and contracts, and the like. Fakes are a fine exemplar of what might be termed the "land-mine." You, as a collector paid for a piece; it is yours. You discover it is a fake. You do not want it to be yours. It is not the mine you believed you had purchased. Does the dealer or auction house reclaim ownership? Must you go to court to rid yourself of this mine? If you possess legal chops, try to outguess the outcome. But I can assure you, universal success in doing so is not likely.

Or suppose an antique was promised to you but the dealer reneged and sold it to someone else (the one you put a verbal hold on at a show). Is a that verbal contract binding (usually not)? Hell has no fury like a collector deprived of what he assumed was going to be a "mine." Of course, if we resided in a perfect world disputes about what is mine would not exist. But irrationalities and strong feelings that are often negative (think of spite) are omnipresent in the collectors' universe.

Sometimes strong values, ethics, and personal emotional commitments enter the world of possession. Can someone make a profit off of past slavery or the Holocaust? Is it proper that Caucasian owners sell to Caucasian collectors and profit from Black slavery ephemera or pieces slaves crafted? Should Nazi items from prior to and during World War II be offered for sale? What are the ethics of selling Native American artifacts? Loud voices and strongly held beliefs may cause pieces to be taken off the marketplace even if collectors of them value their history and believe we should not forget the past. In recent times, the pressures evolving from new ethical constructs have led museums to de-accession collections stolen or bought from nations in Africa, the South Pacific, Eurasia and the Americas. These voices of protest may or may not come from within the collecting community; nonetheless, they can be both loud and convincing. There are times you (or others) may not want something to be yours, no matter how enticing it may be.

Ambiguous feelings about ownership are more common than you might think. If you doubt me, recline your seat on your next flight and have the person sitting behind you protest. Whose space is that 4 inches of space (now 2 inches on many flights)? The airlines actually sell that space twice: once to the seat ticketholder who has the recline button at hand, and once to the person sitting behind her. The conflicts are endless. Who gets to use the center armrest? You have a window seat but I, in the same row want to look out the window. And we are not limited to commercial flying. Did you just steal that parking space while I was shifting into reverse, take the last roll of toilet tissue during a pandemic shopping spree, peek at my answers during an exam? Our conception of what belong to use by right is boundless, as are our feelings when our expectations are frustrated.

"Mines," also reflect the belief that we, as collectors, are not patsies. I think that this self-identity underlies some of the angst about what we will do with our collections someday. We don't want to give them away, have them "stolen" from us, or simply see them disappear into the museum or anonymity. Our goods are valuable both in money and their historic significance. We'll be damned if we are going to be dupes as we dispose of them. For years *Maine Antique Digest* had a monthly column devoted solely to auctions and auction houses. They had one theme, to be blunt: How to avoid being a chump when selling items or an entire collection at auction. Objects that we own (mines) are hardly entirely free of personal emotions.

Possession fills a deep well of self-interest. In many venues paid line-standers appear, and not just at shows or auctions or first-run movies or ticket booths for rock concerts and Broadway but even for entry to the United States Supreme Court. The process is simple. For a fee someone waits in line, sometimes for hours, for you so that you can arrive just as the doors open. I have not yet seen this phenomenon at a prestigious antique show but imagine its presence is only a matter of time. Show promoters may want to ban the practice now.

Additionally, nearly every collector has been near the front of a line at an antique show, headed directly to a dealer's booth he likes, and seen a sold sign on a piece he was serious about purchasing. First come, not first served in this case.

And while we would like to believe that possession is nine tenths of the law (not always by the way), what does possession truly mean and what are its responsibilities? I once visited the archives of Colonial Williamsburg, a huge, climate-controlled building with more storage bins and pieces than I could imagine. Every one of those antiques belongs to Colonial Williamsburg. Yet the homespun blanket I viewed (my wife and I were with the weaver) had only seen the light of day once in decades, for the weaver knew of its existence. I am confident that once the drawer was closed it was unlikely to again see the light of day for yet more decades

Self-Reflection Isn't Just for Self

Like many museums with pieces in collections to study, some of which may be part of an exhibit once in our lifetime, what is the institution's responsibility to all of these "mines" they own? Of what use are all those antiques if they cannot be viewed, enjoyed, and admired by others? There is something odious about having and not sharing at least a glimpse of precious treasures, and museums ought to adopt an ethic that makes <u>access</u> an institutional priority. Recently some have been putting the objects online for viewing and study, a step in the right direction.

I have often wondered about what I think of as a "temporary mine" in the world of American antiques. In the relatively new sharing economy people want to own less. What would happen if ownership had a time limit, if I could lease certain American antiques to grace my home for a year, for example? We think of ownership as permanent, but it does not have to be and sometimes should not be.

In the end, each collector, must work out for himself what his possessions mean to him. In my case, my identity is as a caretaker. I assume my collection will be sold at auction someday, giving other collectors and interested parties a chance to purchase what they want to be theirs. As a caretaker I share my collection with interested folks, and care for the pieces as best I can. You may view your possessions differently. They certainly bring a great deal of meaning and joy to our lives, and sometimes unanticipated complications and unsettling feelings as well.

It is useful to consider what owning antiques truly entails and actually means.

Chapter 18

Notes on a Pandemic: What I Will Never Again Take for Granted

Thornton Wilder's quintessentially American play *Our Town*, first presented in 1938, depicts an American small town, Grover's Corners, New Hampshire, in the early 20th century and the daily lives of its residents. The play is powerful (Wilder would win a Pulitzer Prize for drama). Its central themes: We live life without really appreciating what life has to offer. Once we die, and we are able to see what we had, it is too late. These themes resonate with collectors of American antiques. For it is the simple things in our lives as collectors that we take for granted but that we should treasure. These simple pleasures of collecting life pass us by, typically unappreciated and unnoticed.

In *Our Town*, the narrator assists others in looking back on their lives from beyond the grave. Happily, we can look back at our normal lives from inside our self-quarantine, semi-quarantine, or newfound freedoms, depending on COVID's prevalence and variants. We do not know if this will be the only self-quarantine, the first of several, the first of many, or the initiation of a new life. How much of our former collecting life may be gone forever?

The question a simple one: What are the simple joys of collecting we never fully appreciate until they are denied to us? I have thought some of what these pleasures are. I know that I will take great delight in them once society returns to "normal." (When I first wrote this I was still in self-quarantine and now my life has returned to a semblance of normality. My predictions proved to be true . . . so far).

What surprises and informs me – after all it has only been a few months since the virus changed how we relate and behave in our society – is how much I think about the way collecting was only a month or two ago, and how much I already miss the good old days. What is informative to me is that the needs I meet collecting must be strong and important indeed to cause me to lament their passing so soon after my self-quarantine began. Of course, missing the way things were so recently helps me keep them alive.

Do not get me wrong. Dealers and auction houses are doing yeoman duty for collectors, despite or because of concerns about buying, selling, and diminished revenue. I enjoyed the half- and full-page dealer ads in the antique publications in glorious color. They reminded me what we used to read in such periodicals before dealers turned to the internet. Websites are being added to and updated, and I have received several email blasts from dealers. On-line shows were and are ongoing. Dealers are reaching out to clients and sales are being made. But somehow none of these efforts can make up for the simple pleasures of collecting I miss so very much.

Like many or most collectors once confined to home I continued to do what I could as a "gatherer of antiques." I bid at an on-line auction. I watched Instagram tours of dealers' shops and even purchased a piece featured I read *Maine Antique Digest* and *The Bee* (*Antiques and the Arts Weekly*) in print and on-line. I followed the *Americana Hub* on Facebook. But I find that these distanced activities do not sustain or fulfill me. There are numerous reasons I and others collect, many not related to adding pieces to a collection, and most of these motivations and pleasures are denied to collectors (and dealers) while cooped up at home.

I miss being around people – need I say more? For example, I will never take for granted or complain again about waiting in line for an antique show to open. I felt a pressing need to stay connected with others during the height of the virus, emailing, calling good friends and acquaintances, Skyping or using Zoom. Often there was little to say. We all shared the phenomenon of struggling to know what day of the week it was, our activities circumscribed, novice experts on masks and hand washing. The need for others, to belong, to connect, is powerful and omnipresent. I found such "distant" connections, although clearly better than nothing, did not truly meet my need for interpersonal connectedness. However detailed an email exchange with a dealer, I do not feel the anticipation I feel waiting in line for a show to open.

Even though when using telecommunication, I can hear someone's tone of voice or see their facial expressions, I miss being with the person on the other end of the ether. I miss leaning over at a show during a quiet moment, talking with a dealer about a piece she has for sale. The same holds for learning more about it, negotiating cost, finding out how the dealer has been, thanking her for saving the piece for me to look at, for thinking of me. All of that can be done on-line but the experience, at least for me, is different somehow, not as powerful, as real. It does not meet my needs the way being with someone in person does.

Consider a queue for an antique show. Have we truly appreciated as collectors all that it entails? Muted conversations about everything under the sun – the weather, sports, the dealers, our current collections, vivid past experiences, successes and failures, a good place for coffee and breakfast, a better place for dinner. As we wait, we gossip about the American antique community, for it truly is a small village and everyone seems to know everyone and their business. I am not sure gossip can be luscious unless done with someone else in person – the state of the market, what pieces are going for, the latest auctions or upcoming ones and what pieces sold for and what went unsold, the venue we are waiting to enter, parking, the cost of the ticket, did you get a free ticket? All banal I know, but such conversations are one of the simply joys of being a collector that I cannot wait to experience again.

And then there is the *frisson* attendant on being at a show. If the show is a good one the line begins forming early. Those at the front of the line watch the tail of standees grow. The conversations tend to take place with lowered voices. But as the opening time draws near, the conversations seem to become louder – dare I use the word cacophony? – and the

Self-Reflection Isn't Just for Self

hubbub is noticeable if one simply listens. And the feeling, if a morning show people early in line are just awakening, tired, their coffee not yet washing them into this new day. But as the opening time draws near, the energy of those in line is palpable! Collectors at the starting block, waiting to fall in love or be disappointed, wanting to spend money, wanting to lust, caress, have their breath taken away just once more.

The anticipation is intense, a feeling I never have experienced waiting for an on-line show to begin (my apologies to those promoting and overseeing on-line venues). You can see the expectations and hopes in the faces of fellow collectors, and they in yours. To be blasé at a time like that, unheard of.

Whether in an antique show or a dealer's shop, one sense denied to collectors when collecting on-line is the sense of touch. Running one's hand over a table top not necessarily to learn how smooth or crackled the finish is, but to caress it, to connect with the piece, to begin perhaps to fall in love. I believe the sense of touch is under-appreciated when collecting but a central component in the experience. To hold a piece of silver in one's hand, to turn it over, to feel its weight, its balance, its essence. A simple joy of collecting I will never take for granted again. Of course, some genres, such as paintings or samplers, are not touched but the majority of what we collect is. We pull lopers out and lower drop fronts on desks, turn case furniture over to study its originality and construction, pick up candlesticks to look closely at them, examine redware plates in better light, hold dolls to see how much they have been loved in their previous lives. I long to touch once more.

To touch in many ways is to collect. And of course, there is the touching with others, the shaking of hands, the hugs, air kisses or pecks on the cheek, the holding of both hands in yours as you face someone and ask them seriously how he has been. Touch is a basic need, necessary for us, helping us connect with others and with objects. While not a "touchy feely" person, I miss the shaking of hands, the bumping into others at a crowded show. For the sense touch communicates being part of something, of belonging.

One of course listens not just waiting in line for a show to open. Have you ever stopped for a moment or two, or sat down after a first walk through at a crowded show and just listened? I miss hearing collectors say, "Excuse me" as people accidently bump into other. "Did you see the painting in so and so's booth?" Did you find anything; any luck yet? Did you see the price of that (fill in the blank) in _____'s booth?" "Have you run out of funds yet?" "You should go back and buy it, to hell with the cost." "This chicken wrap is really good." "Thank goodness for water." "Couldn't see anything in _____'s booth; it was too crowded." "Oh, I want it, but it truly is beyond my means." "Come look at a piece I am thinking about. I need your opinion."

And more mystical, I miss objects talking to me. I have never really had a piece pictured on a website take my breath away quite like what occurs when I am attending a show or visiting a dealer's shop in person. Oh my! that moment when you know you may have found a piece to truly live with and love forever. "Psst, over here," it whispers. "Look at me." I cherish that feeling of being drawn into a booth by a single piece, approaching it with reverence, my heart beating faster with every slow step. The wanting to connect with it, to find it true, to bond with it.

Of course, there is more to see than objects at an antique show, and I miss what I used to take for granted once again. Have you ever stopped and made a list of what you see at a show? Crowded aisles or empty ones, objects displayed in different ways, the collectors who walk intensely, talk intensely, collect intensely. The couples who walk together, the disappointment when one falls in love and the other does not, the negotiations of collector with spouse or significant other, of collector with dealer. Those who walk leisurely. Those casually dressed in shorts, those spiffier. Dealers casually dressed, dealers who always wear a suit or dressy outfit. Small bags of purchased items, a short queue at the shipper, the hard floor (it always seems to be so at indoor show), people resting. The increasing age of collectors, sobering for the future of the marketplace. Smiles, frowns, perplexed looks, anxiety, pleasure, happiness, sorrow – the universe of human emotions.

Visiting a dealer's shop is something I truly took for granted. Hours were posted for those dealers who still had a shop and all I had to do was show up. I miss the ambiance and rituals. Coffee and cookies often available, (now we are in the realm of the sense of smell) or something a bit stronger on a quiet afternoon, good conversation, pieces to look at for the first time or again. Typically, wooden floors, the story of how a piece was acquired or the history of that piece over there. I find dealers' shops part of the soul of collecting and to be denied that soul has been disheartening, dangerous to my being almost. Again, gathering information or visiting a shop on-line seems different, less fulfilling than being there.

Of course, during these difficult times, I cannot share my antiques with others if they are interested in looking at them. Rain checks for a visit are given. There was no sitting around our Queen Anne table for a Passover Seder. If someone wanted my opinion on a piece they own, that visit also had to be delayed. A class about antiques, postponed. So many facets of being a collector put on hold and lost.

Perhaps I am a romantic. If so, I wear the label proudly. I hope I am not waxing nostalgic and that the "good old days" will return soon. But the pandemic has reminded me again why it is I collect. If I can hold these thoughts and feelings in consciousness, I will be better for it. I need to remember and hang on to what it is I miss so dearly, so that when they return, and they will, I do not take them for granted the way I once did.

Collecting has proved to be, denied its atmosphere, a world denied, remembered and yearned for.

Chapter 19

Occam's Razor: Collector Happiness or Fulfillment

My dad had a best friend, Sol, whose life he saved in World War II. Not in battle, mind you, but right here in the States. Like dad, Sol was from Chicago, and both were members of the same tribe (Jewish). Sol was scheduled to be shipped out to tail-gunner school. It was an occupation with a life expectancy shorter than a wildly underpriced antique. My dad finagled Sol's appointment to a permanent non-combat position. Their friendship survived the war.

Years later, they would argue good-naturedly about what was important in life. My memory is sketchy, but I remember it was fulfillment that Sol sought. "A bit of happiness," my dad would reply "would suffice for me." I thought of them the other day, both deceased for years, and wished I had been able to partake of the discussion myself. But maybe I can do it now. Is the core of collecting about happiness or fulfillment, perhaps a bit of both, and other feelings as well?

Their back-and-forth conversations over the years reminded me of my teaching days, especially the debates regarding the relative influence of heredity and environment on an individual's intelligence. For decades that debate was framed as nature <u>versus</u> nurture, with researchers on either side attempting to make their case. As it turns out (and is true of many personality traits, not only intelligence) the truth is that innate character and upbringing each contribute about 50%. Surprising how many either/or arguments end up that way.

To resolve the conundrum, I fall back on the proposition that collecting involves both joy and satisfaction – a "bit of both" thesis. Collectors become what they are and continue to be such because their encounters – learning, spending, traveling, losing out, meeting others of their sort, furnishing, attending shows – somehow address something deep within their character, filling and maybe even overfilling a need. I would go even further and venture that for new collectors, darting in and out of dealers' shops, driving to small towns and along back roads, making buying decisions, and attending their first few auctions all are great fun. Still, they will only remain collectors if it begins being more than fun but also tickles their need for personal fulfillment.

In almost every instance, happiness is elusive and cannot be attained directly. One cannot set out to be happy and then just do whatever – buy a new car, raise her bowling score, paint the Mona Lisa, sit back and be forever elated. Happiness is, to be unscientific, an itch. It is temporal and cannot be permanently alleviated by one scratching session. While some philosophers hold that the moral goal of life is happiness, others see it comes to us due to chance. Interestingly, the term happiness in most European languages is a synonym for luck. The Brits are famed for reacting to a positive outcome as due to "happy chance," what we'd call good luck. In other words, we at times find ourselves happy, yet holding onto the feeling is nigh impossible. That feeling of content, pleasure, cheer, or joy, sometimes giddiness, cannot be experienced for long. Happiness is fleeting.

As is true of all emotions, joy involves a cognitive component. We feel happy when we focus on a love, or a glittering moment, or a moving experience, and are surprised to discover we are indeed happy. But do note: Concentration, even such a mundane thing as analysis, is involved. Happiness is not mindless. The feeling is subjective and idiosyncratic. And it is immutable: difficult to communicate to others in objective terms. The swain proposes, she says, "Yes." He breaks into laughter. She asks, "Why are you laughing?" He replies, "Because I am happy." "Why?"

queries the maiden, and he shakes his with a muffled, "Oh, you know." Ah, but she doesn't and can't. It is his happiness. It is beyond words, though I imagine he could try explaining it. I am reminded of Eleanor Roosevelt's observation that "Happiness is not a goal. It's a by-product of a life well lived." Words failed even her.

Fulfillment on the other hand presupposes you and I find that what we do brings a sense of purpose in life. The collector wants to own a particular 18th century blue-and-white Chinese bowl, and by dint of research, diligence and assertive bidding manages to get a prime example for her collection. While the success may induce a temporary elation, the acquisition has long-term effects, a feeling that one has somehow wrested success from adversity, or at least indifference. Fulfillment is more permanent than happiness when one experiences it. Fulfillment brings silence. Fulfillment is deeper than happiness. It lasts. For the collector of American antiques, achievement may not bring this sense. The realization a collector is part of a community, that there are others who share his values, that he has done something to preserve a precious part of our heritage, however, may do so.

Noble, even romantic rhetoric aside and ideals be damned, let me try to draw a clearer distinction between happiness and fulfillment. In many ways, happiness is something that is given to you based on <u>what</u> you do, and fulfillment grows from the satisfaction as to <u>why</u> you do it. The former Is rather random, as much as we may pine for it. The latter also somewhat random as we may do something (raise a family, our work, collect) for some time before we realize those things bring a feeling of fulfillment. We may be surprised to discover they do. We did not set out to be fulfilled but find we are, again a sense of randomness.

Let's creep into the mind of an antique dealer for a moment. Ask him, "Do you like your work?" If he says, "Yes," ask why. An antique dealer may love the feeling of American pieces 200 years old. He loves meeting people at shows, the seeking of new inventory. Connecting collectors to objects they covet makes him smile. He is happy he ended up in this profession. But if you push him as to <u>why</u> he is an antique dealer, perhaps after some thought he may tell you because he believes that history of our nation should be preserved, that if we forget history our lives are shallower. His blogs and conversations with other dealers and collectors emphasize the place of objects in our lives, the critical place of material culture. If he had a slogan it might read, "I keep history alive" or "My mission in life is to keep the history of Connecticut's craftsmen, objects, and culture alive and appreciated." The reasons he is an antique dealer, the whys, bring fulfillment to his life. The fact he is fulfilled allows him to be passionate about it all.

What about collectors then? While I don't mean to dodge the issue, speculating about "the collector's" motivation involves the sort of self-reflection I find uncomfortable, baring my soul a little more than I would like. It also requires temerity. Am I representative? The obvious answer is a blunt "no," but the exercise may provoke you into a similar experiment.

Like so many people, the way I was raised inclined me to value fulfillment (goal orientation) and to pooh-pooh happiness (romantic posturing). Oh, do note the parenthetical expressions, since they are the twaddle of daily life. My maternal grandmother, born in Brooklyn, went on vacation to the Old Country (Poland one day, Russia the next, depending on who was claiming the border) as a young girl, visiting relatives. The "vacation" lasted for 15 years. Grandma's shtetl grandparents and other family were firm in their belief. If life is too good, God will give you misery to balance things out. She not only adopted that ethos but passed it down to her daughter. I was raised to believe happiness is but one hesitant step from disaster.

On the other hand, having a purpose in life fits being Jewish like a fine suit. God does not take fulfillment away like he does happiness. We are remembered for what we did while alive, maybe leaving the world a slightly better place. High ambitions aside, my character has been affected by the belief. I am fully capable of delight – as compatriots can testify, having seen me puff up with joy having helped my team win in a trivia contest. But fulfillment is my cup of tea, and it sits there, steaming, as I collect.

How, as a collector, do I experience pleasure? We (my wife and I), like so many, were introduced to collecting by mentors Bernice and Jim Miller. Collecting ties me to them, people my wife and I cared a great deal for, and we keep their memory and affection alive through our collecting.

My parents also collected, not antiques, but art. Collecting has given us a community tied together by memories, values and – above all – affection.

Still, the very act of being an involved collector has its roots in fulfillment, not only of my personal goals, but of others' expectations. I have long written about the hobby, pounding out thousands of words on who collectors are and what collectors do and what lingers in dusty corners (physical and mental), waiting to be brought back into the light. I am obliged to live up to an alleged expertise. I am expected to "know" what others do not. The very act of probing the mind and behaviors of my fellow collectors and myself is fulfilling in the same way building my own collection has been.

So, delight or satisfaction, happiness or fulfillment, nature or nurture? As always, I can only wish the answer were simpler. To a large measure, the right answer depends on the individual. Speaking personally, I am more motivated by a sense of potential meaning (the why) than by a vague hope for a thrill (the what). Collectors often start their careers with one startling moment, and I would be willing to bet, if asked, most of them could identify not only the object but the occasion (and if not as ancient as I, even the date) when the antique came to hand. That pleasure launched them on a lifetime commitment. But, digging deeper, if the sense of learning, sharing and refining their taste and knowledge didn't slowly grow over time and become a lever that moved them forward, I think they would turn in another direction and leave antique collecting behind, another of those momentary passions that all of us have had in our lives. Some call them fads, others self-deception. I say all that because I have known not a few people – entirely respectable, likeable, intelligent people – who have followed exactly that path. Delight comes and goes, commitment born of fulfillment does not.

Lest I sound too Pollyanna-ish, not all that collecting entails bears positive feelings or glorious experiences. I have been at outdoor shows in mud and rain, feeling as if I was exploring the Amazon or deepest Africa. Some of the people with whom I have had contact – dealers, fellow collectors – were not the nicest people, or the most honest, or the type I would choose to spend time with . . . and didn't. The learning process has been painful on occasion, with no one to blame but myself after overpaying for a piece or buying something I realized later I didn't really want at a fair price (I should have walked on). But these moments remain in the minority. Rita Mae Brown, a well-known author is quoted as saying that "One of the keys to happiness is a bad memory." There are times I am sure I am following her advice.

As for the title of this little exercise, I believe Occam's razor (also spelled Ockhamm or Ocham) is both instructive and apropos: The simplest explanation is usually the right one. When it comes to collecting, we enter the market with both glittering hopes and a sensible plan. Not everyone can own the Star of India, or the Mona Lisa or, for all that, a perfect piece of Paul Revere silver. But that is precisely the point, isn't it? If <u>everyone</u> could, there would be no sense in collecting. The mere possibility, the chance discovery, the reasoned and patient search – oh, and the chance to share this with others – lies at the root of what we do. Listen to the stories collectors tell, their excitement and disappointment, triumphs and competition, the relationships formed. Then you will understand the "why" of collecting. They cannot dream of living without them, these experiences that have become part of the fabric of their lives and bring such satisfaction.

I began with a discussion of happiness, fulfillment, and perhaps other feelings as the foundation of collecting. Herein I focused on the former two, but I offer a third leg to the collector's milking stool – aesthetic pleasure, the feeling of contentment when in the presence of beauty. Not quite fulfillment although the feeling may make life worthwhile, not quite giddy joy yet a form of happiness. Occam may need to accommodate another component of collectors' core emotions. Aesthetic fulfillment, even as part of happiness, deserves its own investigation, another time perhaps.

In collecting, what there is on the outside might not be as valuable as what is on the inside.

Chapter 20
Too Much Stuff

My article discussing what collectors might do with their collections struck a chord. Several letters regarding it appeared in *Maine Antique Digest* I received a few emails. The correspondents and my own experience reminded me of an associated problem collectors face: "too much stuff." Though veteran collectors may be concerned about disbursing their accumulation, apparently this does not stop them from adding to what they have. They soldier on, amassing, upgrading, and dipping their toes in genres new to them. For many collectors there can never be "too much stuff" until they lack the space to display and store it, the capacity to enjoy it, or the money to buy it. Then the amount of stuff becomes unreasonably troublesome and cannot be ignored.

I have encountered the problem myself. To better understand, a bit of background is in order. Back when I first taught at Michigan State University, my wife and I visited a colleague's home. He collected Asian antiques and they were everywhere – on walls, floors, tabletops, piled upward. My wife and I came to agreement that when we had a collection, we did not want it spread with such catholicity throughout our habitat.

We now live in a modest home. We enjoy a sparser look and some walls have deliberately been left unadorned (gasp!). To add to our problem, the walls of our staircase from first to second floor have a large patterned floral design on which artwork looks meh. The challenge: Over the

Self-Reflection Isn't Just for Self

decades we have collected enough posters and paintings to fill available wall space. How can we reconcile our appreciation of what we own with the perfectly reasonable wish to display it?

The obvious answer is to declare what we now have as enough. No more room for display. And that would prove a quietus to our collecting hobby for genres that need to be hung on walls. Another would be to assert we have too much, which opens the door to disposing of things we love, but would allow us to pursue new items and continue collecting.

Let us indulge in an exercise. Given the information that follows, which side would you be on?

We have 32 paintings, posters, and prints now on the walls of our home. Three tallcase clocks three other clocks as well as one mirror need their own space. (No, we haven't closed off any windows yet.)

All was copacetic, as the hip used to say, until an online show brought on the crunch. A poster dealer from whom we and our younger son had both purchased items in the past was offering a poster for sale that both my wife and I lusted after. Keep in mind that my wife collects women-in-aviation pieces, including books and posters (her collection of fiction on the topic numbers over 80 volumes). She already had one poster not related to women in aviation, but airplanes themselves, a Pan Am Clipper, a "bird" she loves. At one point we thought of purchasing yet another, poster of a Lockheed Constellation (nicknamed Connie) punching through the clouds, but it was large, we had no wall space, and we did not love the image.

Then lightning struck. What bowled us over recently was a circa 1952 poster of a Connie flying over New York City at dusk. We were in love. Again, it was large, but this image was the one to own. Its condition was near perfect and the poster was rare – the dealer had seen only three in his 30 years in business. We negotiated a price and purchased it. Romance didn't fade but reality reared its ugly head. We had no place to hang it, what were we to do?

To solicit ideas, I posted on the Facebook page, *Americana Hub* (Take a look at the site, you will like it), and collectors and dealers responded with their own stories and suggestions. Collectors are infinitely resourceful, and here are some of the alternatives we were offered.

Several folks recommended we purchase a larger home, assuming more square footage would offer more wall space for art and posters. They had done exactly that to handle their growing collections or knew someone who had. One dealer told me he worked with a client who filled up a 10,000 square foot home, then purchased one twice as large to house continuing acquisitions. Another told me he had a client who built an addition to his home to display one painting. Enticing as the notion was, we were happy in our home, with square footage many baby boomers downsize to, and adopting the suggestion certainly would result in an expensive divorce. Another offered a cautionary tale. A larger home with an open floor plan did not offer more wall space but less. Oh, I was not surprised that one alternative was to increase the space available for the stuff. Collectors would think that way. More stuff needs more space.

The alternative recommendation was a second house. One respondent did just that. His place of work became his second display venue. Even if one sets aside such things as cost, maintenance, deciding whether my wife occupies one and I the other (Did I just mention divorce?), the idea was a non-starter.

A second notion was to upgrade our collection: Place our posters and artwork side by side by side and decide which works we liked least and then sell the latter. The recommendation assumed that for some reason we have never taken a careful look at what we have, or perhaps our tastes have changed, or maybe we're a bit too complacent about what is and is not good in our collection. On the contrary, liking something less does not mean it is disliked. My wife and I probably would have very different opinions of what was to be sold, the charm held by stories attached to each piece, and what we wanted to view and live with. (I hope that knocking I hear is not a lawyer holding a writ.)

It was clear that folks who urged us to sell some pieces thought they were on the right track, although the suggestion overlooked the fact that we were trying to solve our space problem while keeping what we had. Those who opposed such a sale gasped at the, equating it with sending a member of the family off to indentured servitude.

Of course, we could make our space problem a problem for others. We could give this and that to grown children, particularly if they

Self-Reflection Isn't Just for Self

have intentionally or accidentally admired a piece or two in our hoard. Hearing this possibility, admiration and affection soon gives way to their realization that they, too, already have a space problem. Burdening (uh, "gifting") friends in a similar way yields, to no one's surprise, the same result. Lending pieces to a museum or historic society also is an option, but we – like many – either have no such institution at hand, or it does not collect what we want to give, or it already has one of "them," or our pride and joy would go into storage, likely never to be seen again.

One alternative was to be creative where or how the artwork was displayed. People suggested putting art works on wreath stands and perching them on couch tables, hanging them on bookcases (more attractive than the spines of thrillers and murder mysteries), putting them above door frames (though it does screw up perspective, and hanging them on wall space behind doors (you can only see the paintings when the door is closed). We already do the last and have placed several face jugs in a bookcase. Someone said they hang smaller works of art from dresser or cupboard knobs. Another observed that little children and dogs solve the problem; one dare not have much of anything of value hung anywhere. Of course, the works do not have to be hung, someone pointed out. They can lean on the floor against a wall. We already do that, I posted, and I counted four works of art visibly leaning near me as I typed. A floor-to-ceiling design was trumpeted as a solution, but our desire for some blank space preempted stacking paintings one on top of the other from our toes to crown molding. We could of course remove our stairwell wallpaper and put up a plan neutral paper suitable for displaying art. Again, practicality triumphed. One wall backs on the Wisconsin outside, gets cold in winter (no surprise), and the cold cracks paint applied to the plaster. Add to that the fact that we are somewhat older, and the chaos of having the space redone is an experience we would rather not endure. And while I might entertain such a notion, we are back again to my wife's feelings. No, dear, we won't.

The solution we accepted: Rotate our art and poster collection. Doing so had its merits. We were forced to assess what we had, choosing good, better, best. It was interesting to look at what needed to be moved and taken down. Questions arose. Did we really love that piece at one point in time? Why didn't we hang that here to begin with, it looks so much better in this light? Do you think we'll ever rehang that?

An important question: Where do we store what is waiting to be displayed at some future date? Art and posters need to be cared for. We checked with an art dealer about how to pack and store an oil painting. We needed to wrap posters (framed and under glass) to keep dust out but did not want to trap moisture in. We found we had no good place for what was to be stashed away. We investigated a climate-controlled storage unit. but even the smallest of the ones available would be largely empty. Share the unit with someone else, someone opined. We have no one with similar needs that we know. How about a storage unit co-op used by several collectors? A great suggestion but again, no area collectors with whom to do so. One largely unused closet in our house is unheated and gets cold in the winter and more importantly and negatively, extremely hot in the summer, removing it from consideration. Our basement with some heat, the dehumidifier running in the summer, while dusty, proved the best alternative.

Of course, the same problem exists for any collectors' favorite genres. Furniture can be moved around but eventually one runs out of floor space. No wonder the Shakers hung their chairs from pegs. Even small items need a tavern table or other tops to perch on, or display cases, and in time they accumulate and the "too much stuff" syndrome reappears. I know of one pewter collector who ran out of space to display his collection, so he is having a reproduction cupboard constructed, just like an antique one he owns. His home is large enough that he has room for it.

What it all boils down to is I knew that collecting was a challenge but never thought of the demand made by loving and owning too much Americana. To love what we own and be surrounded by its beauty never seemed troublesome until the pieces we found less exquisite had to be relegated to our basement of all places – not forever mind you, but still . . . Looked at more expansively, imagine the challenge faced by well-endowed museums with thousands or tens of thousands of beautiful objects and limited space. They face the same problem we do, multiplied by a factor of ten.

Self-Reflection Isn't Just for Self

I had a dear friend who because of dementia needed assisted living. His room contained a few American antiques he had lived with his entire life and which his grown children thought resonated with him still – a cupboard that stood in the kitchen for decades, two Windsor chairs, objects that were utilitarian in his one-room apartment and that provided comfort and memories for him. How lucky he was to have part of his life with him still. "Stuff" is actually memories, feelings, or own past. It is not readily or easily disposed of or dispensed with.

With stuff in storage, I am curious what I will miss and what I will remember only when I discover it months from now, wondering why I had any difficulty at all in taking it down and stowing it. We have already found that some paintings and posters in new locations look fresh to us once again, at least one benefit of culling "too much stuff." You might wonder what piece is first in line to grace a wall when we rotate our art. John Badger Bachelder's map and panoramic view of the Battle of Gettysburg, commissioned by the Army in 1863, displays the topography and location of every unit. It currently leans against one of our rope beds. Next time it will be on the wall. As for the next piece to be taken down and stored away? As Hamlet said, "Aye, there's the rub."

Since we collectors seem to never stop collecting, let me know how your winnowing and sifting progresses and what insightful methods you have found for weeding your antique garden. As for me, if only that Bachelder was smaller, there may be a space behind another door . . .

Collectors must resign themselves to confronting abundance without sacrificing delight.

Chapter 21

The Fascination With "Top Sellers"

"Reality is merely an illusion, albeit a very persistent one."
                                                    Einstein

You see it so often you probably take it for granted. Auction houses trumpet the few pieces that brought the most dollars, their past achievements, the highest price for the genre, the hits, the sales that surpassed the estimates and kept climbing to rarified heights. I have come to expect a paragraph or two in Americana publications about such notable outliers, always and inevitably accompanied by a photo. One seller's headline brags about a record price. Another highlights a piece that "could" be the top lot. Sometimes even glancing coverage of a show touts the most expensive piece to leave the floor. But why? Why are we fascinated by the most expensive?

The phenomenon is not solely the purview of the American Antiques' world. It is common in genres from classic cars to watches to coins.

Is all this to convince us – maybe even themselves – the market is booming and that buyers should, must pile in? Is it intended to engender hopes in the collector that something he owns will prove a Golconda? Should she perhaps anticipate finding a chair just like it for pennies in some dusty corner of an out-of-the-way shop? Or is it a marketing strategy? It seemed time to put on my psychologist hat and delve deeper in the highest price phenomenon.

And so, I reached out to Clayton Pennington, editor of *Maine Antique Digest* hoping for some insight. In brief, he said,

> ". . . I suppose that the highest priced objects in the auction are automatically newsworthy. Top earners get the highlights of the sales that we report on. I wonder about this too sometimes. On *MAD*'s Instagram, objects that blew away estimates always get the most interest/clicks/likes. Some great and interesting stuff is often ignored. More expensive is sexy, I guess."

Clayton confirms my suspicion that something is going on here. But why more expensive is sexy remains elusive. Greg Smith, editor of *The Bee* emphasized collector "education and longing" as lurking behind this emphasis on the supposed best-of-the-best. The confounding fact remains: Collectors can find fulfillment, satisfaction and even pride in owning pieces that others would consider flops or second-quality or pedestrian. They don't need the most expensive to be happy,

Publications that cover the American antique market are chronicles, keeping track of what is trending or doing well at the moment. It makes sense then that they spend time on top-lot pieces. Their reporting may drive tastes, prices and even aesthetics. But we must remember that they are – at least are supposed to be – no more than reporters of the facts, not shills for certain periods, categories or dealers. Anyone who has collected for a while recognizes precisely how cyclical the market can be. Hot sellers appear and vanish in these snapshots. Rising tides do not lift all boats. Yet when we are interested in the sterling price for a Windsor chair, it does not mean the ones I own are suddenly worth more or much more. Publications give us information, tickle our fancy, but are mere verbal or visual histories.

Is this practice of emphasizing high prices a source of fantasy for collectors? In order to get an answer, my wife and I wandered through our pieces. Easy, right? Out of all the objects we possess one poster may meet the "potential top lot" criteria. We have owned *Across the Pacific*

The Fascination With "Top Sellers"

in Five Days Via Pan American for 25 years. The poster pictures the Pan Am Clipper (airplane) and we bought it from well-known dealers who had purchased it from a museum that deaccessioned it. Its condition is perfect. It was never folded. The colors are as bright as the day it was printed. We decided it would be nice if it set a record price. The piece simply deserves recognition of that sort. If it only did "okay" and not "terrific" at an auction, I would not morosely drink good Scotch to console myself. The enjoyment we get from the poster is what is important, not the value someone else would place on it. So, fantasy? Naw.

Someone else with whom I talked wondered whether watching high prices was a form of voyeurism. It struck me that this idea might have some validity. I recall the movies from the 1930s, amidst the Depression. There was Fred Astaire in his top hat and tails, women in beautiful dresses, always in expensive settings – penthouses, exotic locales, staterooms in ships bigger than most people's homes. The flicks let people forget their financial woes. They could clothe themselves in images the flickering bulb was shaping, dream perhaps that it could be them ordering cocktails, or dancing backwards in high heels. Do rich values carry us away from our somewhat mundane lives, carry us into the If-Only world of fantasy? Are stratospheric prices no more than momentary entertainment? A possibility for sure.

Yet another possibility is that these extraordinary sales numbers help train our eye to tell the difference between the good and the superb. If so, we need to find other ways of learning. With rare exception, winners are not described in great detail. We do not know their condition, what their characteristics really are. I remember a piece of furniture that sold at auction for over $100,000. I loved the form, but the surface looked redone. It was its form and dimensions that made it a killer piece, but any collector who valued an original surface would have passed. Record setters are not always best in a genre. No matter what else, collectors can decide rarity, value and condition, just as it should be.

Keep in mind that all it takes is the consignor's dream coalition to push a piece to great heights at auction. I speak of two bidders both of whom have decided the object must be theirs. A war is being fought. The victor may well own the top lot in an auction. Even then, there is no assurance that the towering price is justifiable, explicable, even reasonable.

Behavioral economics also offers an insight into the phenomenon – Irrational Value Assessment, sometimes called the Marketing Placebo or Price/Quality effect. Something certainly is going on when a phenomenon has three different labels. Simply put, the notion holds the more expensive good is always qualitatively better. A Rolex watch used by racers might bring a quarter-million at an auction, and surely one would think that signified a noble, valued timepiece. That same watch, once worn by Paul Newman and bearing an inscription from his loving wife sold for $17.5 million. Which one was the Best? Bluntly, they were identical except for that little grace note: owned by the famed. Students who pay full price for a sugar-rich drink with caffeine and are told that it improves their focus and alertness in the short term outperform peers (by 30%) who were given the same soda at a discount price. In other words, psychologically cheaper is inferior. In some markets and one hates to admit antique collecting may be one of them, there is an indelible blurring between price and quality.

As humans, we are biased toward the dear, partly because more costly things are also rarer and harder to possess. What is fascinating about the research is that the beliefs, choices, and behaviors are unconscious and when asked, research participants do not point to price as influencing their decisions or behavior. Sometimes we read about a piece at auction that was bought well, but such information is usually buried and few auction houses run ads highlighting pieces that were good buys for collectors.

We also associate higher prices with lower risk. Thus, the decision to buy a really expensive antique is thought less risky one because it seems to have inherent value and attraction for others (someone smart bought it for a lot, right?).

To the extent that vicariously indulging in following high-price antiquities is entertaining, it is also intensely social, as I noted earlier. I speak of gossip. "Did you see what that painting went for?" "Why would someone pay that much?" Gossip is delicious and since the American antiques community is small it not only reverberates but bonds collectors.

The Fascination With "Top Sellers"

Importantly, gossip and talking about top lots allows us to enter a world we are not a part of. But through our gossip and conversations we can participate at a distance. And again, socialization plays a part. Others agree with us. We cannot find someone who would have paid what that piece brought.

While gossip typically has a negative connotation, it also can be positive. It may force us to assess our own values and beliefs. Are there antiques I would really rob a bank to own? It may help us gauge or own social standing and successes. I remember once talking to a friend in line for the New Hampshire Dealers' Show. He asked me what I was willing to spend if I fell in love with something. I told him. The amount was higher than he could afford. Interesting, I thought to myself, Time to stop kvetching about what is beyond your means and give thanks for what you can afford. Frankly, there is a pleasure in being envied, and you can hardly discount that as a motive for paying through the nose.

Let's turn our attention to the "overpriced" objects themselves. Certainly, there are times when top lots <u>do</u> represent the best of collecting, expensive because the craftsman who made them centuries ago captured a sense of proportion, beauty, creativity, and perhaps whimsy that has stood the test of time. It is far too easy to dismiss the price paid for a piece as being out of line. In more than one case, that assignation is purely subjective. If your entire budget is $10, spending a buck on a soda seems excessive. If you make two-hundred-fifty grand annually . . . you get the point.

Never forget: There are rewards in owning something wonderful, even if it is mighty expensive. One of them is that it reflects back on you. Ask anyone who owns a Rolls Royce, even though a Toyota would do the job. Or a Rolex. It is far more than inspiring envy in others. The object itself, its quality, its very perfection stirs the soul. You'd be surprised how many stratospherically-priced baubles disappear from public view, only to be cherished by the owner and a few friends (and if you doubt me, study the odd history of the Hope diamond).

As always, the reason top-dollar purchases attract and fascinate are multiple and intersecting. Whatever causal theory you settle on, don't forget to appreciate and cherish the antiques themselves.

"Top Sellers" are a magnet for our attention. Enjoy but beware.

Section IV

Lessons
(Sometimes Waiting to Be Learned)

Chapter 22

Auctions and Collectors: The Psychology of Our Bidding (Often More Than We Had Planned)

Auctions are one of the primary means by which American antiques are sold. I have eagerly awaited auction catalogs, attended previews, bid at auctions, and purchased and lost out at them. Auctions can be great theater but a successful auction for a consignor or auction house may not thrill all collectors. They think, The prices, oh my – that someone was willing to pay that much. Let's look at what auction houses do to attract and sell to us, collectors of Americana, and what influences our bidding, including our own irrationalities and biases. Much of what follows applies to all auctions, but the emphasis is on those that take place with bidders in attendance at the auction house (as well as online).

The auction house's goal: To influence collectors' thoughts and feelings so a large number sign up to bid, and that many do so and do so robustly. To build anticipation, energy, excitement, and buzz – collectors saying to themselves and other collectors thinking, Strong pieces, going to be some spirited bidding, so there are items I am interested in. The auction house wants to grab a collector's attention, and if the stars align, it hopes that many collectors are caught up in the moment. The collector says, "What the heck, I'll pay (or paid) a bit more than I thought but it sure is worth it." And has a great story to tell about the piece(s) purchased (or not) at that great auction.

A number of auction houses are known for their sales of American antiques. Sure, American antiques may not be their prime source of revenue. Truth be told, for many auction houses the American antiques division is an outlier, bringing in far less revenue than other departments. To be labeled a "sale of American antiques" the auction house needs different genres, bringing collectors who specialize in each, increasing the pool of bidders and hopefully (from the auction house's and consignors' perspective) bidder vying against bidder.

Quality pieces create a cachet and attract collectors with thicker wallets, museums and other institutions, and dealers either bidding for inventory or representing clients. Collectors conclude: This is a strong auction of Americana. This is an auction I want to attend. The pieces are quality so the one(s) I am interested in are quality as well. (More on this logic later.)

Auction houses seek to build a reputation, so collectors say to themselves, Fantastic pieces once again. Their auctions are special. Auction houses know that rising tides lift all boats. If blockbuster pieces sell for strong prices, collectors may pay more for other items. Auctions often result in the sale of pieces for more than dealers are asking for comparable or better examples in their shops. I am not sure the collector really is aware this is transpiring. In a group situation we often lose sense of our own individuality and are carried along by the crowd, in this case other auction-goers, a phenomenon known as social facilitation.

Marketing creates awareness and excitement. Auction houses are weavers of dreams. Phone calls are made to important customers, full page color ads and articles about the up-coming auction appear, as will a catalog with wonderful photographs and item descriptions. Perhaps there is a presentation by an expert or a round table the night before the auction takes place. Previews provide a chance to finger goods, eyeball them, long and lust. In print ads for auctions, typically pieces are shown at various price points. The auction house wants the collector who is looking for affordable items as well as those willing to spend a great deal.

Social media and the Internet are useful media to build interest, and grab the collector. Photographs and descriptions of pieces on Facebook or Instagram herald the upcoming auction. Pieces are labeled "Exceptional," "Iconic," "Remarkable," "Best," "Important," "From the collection of," "Legendary," "First time on the market in . . .," "Rare," "Similar to one in the ____ museum," "Crafted by ____." Such adjectives, and the pieces that live up to them, whet the appetite, create attention, and may bring strong bids. The goal is to get a collector thinking to herself, I am interested in the auction, waiting for the catalog online or ordering one, attending a preview in person if possible or having someone do so for me. I am setting aside dollars for this auction.

The piece may be flawed, it may not be great, but collectors need to know the strengths and weaknesses of items they are bidding for. Auction houses provide descriptions, sometimes detailed, especially if the piece is an important one. The catalog description may take up an entire page or more, for other pieces, a line or two.

Are you still uncertain whether the item and condition description is complete? Turn to the online button to ask for additional condition reports or pick up the phone and talk with someone. I have heard of consignors writing their own item descriptions so they are ensured of accuracy. Sometimes someone not at the auction house may be hired to do the job, but typically the seller provides item descriptions from the appraisal, and the auction house adds, changes, or accepts them. The goal once again is a collector thinking, I know what I am going to be bidding on, the piece's strengths and relative weaknesses. I have confidence in the auction house's integrity.

Of course, an erroneous description may lead to collector ecstasy. That painting described as "in the manner of" may be by the noted artist himself, the piece of furniture misattributed. The piece described as English is really American and a buyer hopes she is the only one who knows so.

The goal of the auction, of course, is to bring the consignor and auction house high prices, and to sell as many pieces as possible at those strong prices. It does no one any good, except the purchaser, if good pieces sell for a song. And the order of pieces in an auction, those pictured in a catalog and those merely described, those grouped and those

Lessions (Sometimes Waiting to Be Learned)

listed individually, is no accident (at least some of the time). Sometimes a blockbuster piece is sold early on to build energy and the conclusion by collectors: Prices will be strong. Sometimes to build anticipation the great piece or two placed in the middle of the auction, collectors waiting, those at the phones waiting, everyone waiting. The goal: To build tension, a collector noting, look at all those phones in play.

Oftentimes similar pieces are not sold one after another (quilts seem an exception, or oriental rugs that frequently seem to appear at the end of auctions). A drop-front desk may go early in the auction, another 45 minutes later, another a half hour after that. Miss out on the first one and you have another chance. If they are grouped together the collector may not even notice; one looks like the next. At specialist auctions, stoneware or jewelry pieces, of course, follow one after another.

Some grouping of items makes sense. Who wants to sit through smalls sold individually? So, kitchen items, marbles, chairs, and so forth are sometimes grouped. I have seen a chair paired with a table. The goal: Keep the auction moving along. Perhaps a collector thinking, Not bad, for the estimate I get seven pieces of pewter, why not?

The bane of an auction house is a consignor who overvalues what he owns (the endowment effect) and asks for reserves that are above what the market will bear. Nothing deadens an auction quite like active bidding only to have items bought in because the reserves were not met. For really good items, a low reserve may actually be an advantage for the owner if the auction house does a good job of marketing.

The goal of reasonable estimates and reserves? Collectors saying, "I have a chance to own that painting I like even if I have to reach a bit," or "This is going to be a fun auction; items are affordable and there are some bargains to be had." The belief that bargains (potentially) exist is a powerful tool for an auction house. Collectors are excited, energetic, and if one is outbid there are other pieces that seem (before bidding begins) affordable.

Collectors' beliefs affect their bidding. A collector may assume: Smaller auction houses often have great deals, or country auctions are the best. I always look for fresh to the market, undiscovered pieces at a country auction. A specialist auction house commands high prices but, of course, it sells the best of the best. Auction houses benefit from this halo effect: The fact that perceptions or realities of quality and prestige in one area spill over and influence purchasing in others. Serious collectors tell themselves, Judge the piece independent of the seller, the locale, the description. Easier said than done sometimes.

If you have been successful at a specific auction house, have been treated well, or resonate with its offerings, you may view its future auctions through rose-colored glasses. You believe the pieces are good, the prices favorable. Such beliefs cause a collector to overlook information to the contrary. In other words, we tend to listen more often to information, and favor that information, if it confirms our prevailing beliefs – the confirmation bias. Our memory of what transpired and the conclusions we draw from past events become our collecting destiny.

Collectors are competitive. In ascending auctions where the bids rise until only one person "wins," one would assume that bidding the "true value" of the piece would be the norm. Yet often times attendees bid more than the true value because they want to win, and experience all of the emotions that we attribute to winning. (As one auctioneer called it, "Beating up on others.") While not rational (again, who said we were rational beings?) we will be damned if we will let "that person" or anyone else beat us out. In other words, we end up (enthusiastically) overpaying. Pogo's classic quote comes to mind. "We have met the enemy [of fair prices] and he is us."

Contributing to how high we bid, the "endowment effect" also must be considered. In this case a collector may have fantasized being the winning bidder, the object in the dreams he has woven for himself is already his. He, thus, overvalues the piece as reflected in his bidding.

The power of emotion often rules the day. For weeks a collector may have anticipated the satisfaction, relief, and pride from winning a piece and felt the discomfort, regret, sadness, and even anger from losing out. A bidder may desire the object badly and desire overcomes a more rational assignment of worth. The bidder, emotion unchecked, loses himself in the auctioneer's voice, the bidders around him, the spirited emotion in the room (social facilitation). Commonly known as "auction fever" it is the rare auction-goer who hasn't experienced it at least once. The pre-

Lessions (Sometimes Waiting to Be Learned)

determined bidding strategy and what a collector believed he would pay goes out the window.

Another psychological factor affecting bidding is scarcity. The object may be scarce and if the collector asks himself, "When will I ever see another?" this belief may motivate paying too much. Of course, time is scarce as well, in a live auction a bidder has only seconds oftentimes to make a series of complex decisions.

Collectors also need be aware of the phenomenon of "social proof," a phenomenon wherein others' behaviors affect our own. If the bidding is spirited on a piece and the bids are rising rapidly a bidder may assume: The piece is worthwhile, others want it, others have judged its worth positively. The object is important and valuable. Therefore, I want it!

Pleasing others also affects bidding. Need I mention all of the dynamics and forces that enter into a relationship, and how it may affect a collector at an auction. Your spouse asks (tells, suggests, demands) that you bid once more. Despite your misgivings you do so – far wiser than facing the post-auction discussion about "why didn't you . . .?" You have bid against another collector and the bids rise. There is a pause. The auctioneer leans over the podium and looks at you, saying in a pleasing, quiet voice, "One more bid sir, just one more, oh come on, you know you want the piece." Such intimacy.

Auction houses know all the retailing tricks and probably have invented a few themselves. My advice is to do your homework, have fun, get used to not getting what you want, realize you are being "sold," and enjoy your successes. May the auctioneer be looking at you when she says "sold," may the item be special, may the price be fair, and if not, may you not care.

Collectors need to learn about and master buying at auctions.

Chapter 23

Choice

"It's your thing, do what you want to do."
The Isley Brothers

People who collect do so because of what it adds to their lives – relationships, meaning, fun, satisfaction, fulfillment, an aesthetic experience, preservation of the past, an opportunity to be a scholar, and to own lots of objects. They <u>choose</u> to collect, because they are free agents who define themselves and their lives through the choices they make. John-Paul Sartre held that we <u>are</u> our choices.

Existentialists argue that there is no meaning inherent in the universe "out there," but we create what is meaningful for ourselves. For many of us, we know we know that the act of collecting gives meaning to our lives. Some may feel giddy with the ideas of limitless freedom. For others, the notion that we are free to live our lives any way we choose leads to paralysis, dread, and a yearning for external structure and even the need to be guided. Their cry is, "Tell me what to do."

I have collected American antiques for some decades. At times I am overwhelmed by the manifold obligations attendant on collecting – shows I must attend, auction-offerings to peruse, websites to inspect, dealers with whom to keep in touch. Nothing so kills a passion as its becoming less like pleasure and more like labor. I persevere, knowing I am free to cut back on those activities or my collecting altogether, or to begin to collect other genres. I could, of course, choose to redouble my efforts to not miss out on great antiques but I opt not to. I go forward, as most collectors do, because I know I have choices, alternative paths to follow, new knowledge to acquire.

One of my relief valves lies in the time I spend writing about collecting. That particular choice is built on the fact that I love taking pen to paper, cherish manipulating words, and enjoy the challenge of using them to describe collectors' worlds and experiences. While mixing collecting and writing about the hobby takes time, neither usually feels like a burden.

I indulge in a fantasy that following my routine and keeping abreast of what pieces are available through dealers or auctions will result in some sort of triumph: The discovery and possession of an exemplary rarity, a phrase so apt that others choose to admire and quote it. The truth is, occasionally I will find a piece I love and can afford, but oftentimes I will miss out or be disappointed. And no matter how much vigor and polish I apply to my prose, there is always a moment when I consider something I once thought perfectly done and sigh, "dull." Still, I choose to laugh at the situation rather than surrender or descend into despair.

In other words, by giving up the idea that a collector should always win, or win most of the time, I do not spend energy bemoaning the loss of more happy endings in my collecting life. Collecting, like life, consists of a series of compromises: good and bad, order and chaos, luck and loss.

Every collector is free to choose how he collects and how he responds to successes and failures, good buys and bad, too little money, and bad luck. But I must emphasize that my choices are not necessarily right for you. Choice is indelibly individual, a fingerprint of personality.

For some who feel trapped in their collecting, for whom the choice to collect no longer offers them the meaning and satisfaction it once did, or for whom the genres they collect have become too expensive, repetitive or familiar, they may decide to shed the burden. I know of one couple who simply stopped collecting Americana. Their house was full, the thrill of the chase had disappeared, the satisfaction was gone. Because they still liked collecting, they changed genres, shifting attention from American antiques from the early to mid-19th century to a new genre, the "industrial look." When last I talked with them, they were once again happy.

Another couple comes to mind. They also collected American antiques, but at a much higher level than most of us. They had worked with the best of dealers. Their collection embraced exemplary pieces of great rarity and high quality. They had expended impressive sums, year after year. But even with their discretionary dollars, they found American antiques, at least the ones they loved, becoming too expensive. Their decision was an interesting one. Using a prestigious auction house, with a catalog for which they themselves wrote item descriptions, they auctioned off their collection, saving only one or two pieces, and not the best ones at that. Others have done that, you say. True, but they made a second decision I find fascinating. They stayed involved American antique collecting and kept in contact with the dealers and friends they had met and made while collecting. They still attend shows, they schmooze, they walk the aisles, they look, but they do not buy.

In other words, collectors are free to collect or not in ways they choose. The two couples described above made radically different choices and ended up happy. Surely this demonstrates there is no one path, and there is no right path. What is important is what suits a particular collector at that point in his life.

To be free to choose also means being somewhat immune to the exhortations of experts who extol collecting in a certain way. One often hears, "Buy the best that you can afford." I always thought this good advice if one wants to build a collection that amounts to anything. But you don't have to do so. The difficulty in collecting is making the choices, both in terms of the pieces purchased and in how you make decisions.

Knowing we have the ability and freedom to choose, collectors must embrace the notion that it is their collection, and they can put in it what they want. We can read books and blogs, visit museums, solicit advice from dealers, and look at what genres make up noted collections but, in the end, it is our choice on how to proceed and what to buy. I remember years ago when our house was not yet full more than one dealer told us that any collection worth anything (aesthetically, not monetarily) needed a lowboy. My wife and listened carefully and then proceeded to reject that advice, instead purchasing a painted card table to fill the space set aside for one. Another collector would have purchased a lowboy and been thrilled. Our choice was different. "Collect one thing," some say. "A collection should be coherent," others advise. In contrast, our collection marries 18th and early 19th century Americana with objects celebrating my wife's love of women who fly and aviation. We think the fusion of interests and of genres works. Others may disagree, of course, and we are willing to lend them a deaf ear.

Collectors' choices range more widely than just those mentioned so far. They are free to upgrade certain pieces or not, to stick with genres they have been familiar with for decades or to collect something new. It was only recently that I began collecting redware plates with writing on them. Fool that I am, just before I made that decision and purchased my first few examples, they were readily available in the marketplace. Not any longer. In good condition they have become rare or beyond my means. Still, we own a few charmers and I look for more because the genre resonates within me.

I cannot emphasize too strongly the centrality of choice: Every collector is free to amass a collection in the way she chooses. Certainly, it is easier to work with one or two dealers and let their advice, pickers, and inventory determine what your collection becomes. Many have followed this path in the past, often to their complete satisfaction. But pick your path; don't let someone hand you a pre-marked route. Let me add, it is sometimes difficult being all grown up as a collector. If one option facing us is, "Tell me what to do," and following the expert's advice (think of this as partial responsibility), its counterpart is, "I will decide for myself" (full responsibility). You can do both over time, and you can do both at the same time.

Failing to listen to others' experiences built up over years – involving more antiques, dealers, auctions, and collectors than you will experience in a lifetime – would indeed be foolish. But who is more qualified to build your collection than you yourself? There is a lot of hubbub in the American antiques community – opinion, advice, marketing, word of mouth, fables, hucksterism – telling you what to purchase and how to collect. Understanding this, you may allow yourself to be influenced by this chatter – sometimes to your betterment as a collector, and sometimes not – as long as you make decisions with your eyes open and feel you are being true to yourself.

The choices you make may lead to disenchantment. Your collection may end up failing to meet your standards in places. If so, you may need more preparation and education, to improve your connoisseurship, to work with different dealers, to take a break from collecting, to give it up. Or not. Your choice.

The choices we collectors make are many. What to collect? At what price points? From whom do I purchase pieces for my collection? How do I purchase – in person only, from photographs and detailed descriptions, from dealers, from auction houses, from private parties? Do I save all year and buy one great piece if I can find it? Do I simple purchase the first piece I fall in love with? Will I borrow money to get the antique of my dreams? Will I purchase without expert guidance? Do I trust myself enough to buy at Brimfield or a country auction using my own judgment? Depending on the genres I collect, do I want breadth, even if this means average condition for some pieces? Or do I value depth, buying fewer pieces but in marvelous condition? And so it goes. I found that making a list of my collector profile was helpful and useful for me. It may be something you want to do, too.

When deciding the answer to these questions, I had to assess my own habits. I found that I struggle sometimes to wait for a fine piece, instead purchasing average items I end up unhappy with. I purchase in person whenever possible. I will not purchase at auction without an expert's advice if the piece is pricey by my standards. I am most comfortable adding to my collection after conferring with people I trust but will buy at a show without any guidance. Putting items on hold at a show allows me to walk around and think about a piece for a bit. I would rather overpay for an object I love than miss out on it (especially now, given my age) even though I know intellectually as one door closes (I miss out on it and hang onto my money) another opens (another great piece becomes available). The ancient Greek philosophers lived by one ideal: "Know thyself." If it was true 2,500 years ago, it has its own relevance when you are figuring out how to collect.

Lessons (Sometimes Waiting to Be Learned)

Just as I need to know myself, I need to have a firm grasp of the elements in the collection I already own. I need to consider my immediate options: buy, wait, walk away. Is the enticing collectible really worth pursuing if it is in jarring contrast with – or inconsistent with – what I already have? A cautionary tale: I have only found one Windsor bench for a bay in our dining room in over a decade of looking. But I walked away from it because of its surface. I concluded that surface is important to me. Since then, I have pounced on other pieces. I know that the longer it takes to make a decision, the more I can probably live without the item.

Finally, financial considerations seem to sway some of my decisions. Sometimes I wish they would not.

I find myself in a bit of a pickle. If it is true that one of the merits and burdens of being a collector is the power to choose – to say yes or no – is it not also true that the prudent collector should decide whether to take the advice I have so fervently offered? Why should I tell you how or what to collect? Though I prefer you'd think of me as a guide, guru, lama, or sensi bundled in a neat package, I am consoled by the realization that collectors not only have the power to think their way through thorny problems, but they have the inclination to do precisely that. Enjoy the freedom to choose.

Collectors decide how and what they choose to collect.

Chapter 24

The Importance of the Word "Important"

Simply stated, the voice of collectors in the American antiques world has been muffled. Plenty is written expressing the opinions, judgments and prejudices of experts and dealers, and all of these (well, to an extent) have value – some offering brilliant insights, others serving as cautionary tales. But it is mostly collectors who make the market function. They shell out hard-earned (or comfortably inherited) dollars to purchase treasures from dealers and auction houses. Without collectors and their purchasing power, there would be no American antiques' universe. Someone needs to speak for them, their interests, and – yes – their occasional confusion.

Collecting is a fundamentally economic activity: trading money for goods. The wise allocation on our fiscal collecting resources is so important that in my book, *Come Collect with Me*, I devoted an entire section to *Dollars and Sense*. There I noted that our spending is not always rational, not always prudent, and not always informed. As I wrote then, "We are influenced by emotion, suffer self-control difficulties, and are victims of distraction."

This list of mistakes we are tempted to make (and we so frequently give in to temptation) is long. Sometimes we think money is not real. We forget how hard we worked to earn it, especially when it morphs into a plastic credit card. At other times, when given a choice, we pay more than we expected for a piece that was better than the one we had planned on purchasing. And there are market factors that play a part, too. At an auction, as I note in Chapter 22, collectors may throw fiscal caution to the wind, caught in a competitive fever.

There are people out there (never us, of course) who place greater value on what they own than the objects deserve. They foolishly equate high prices with high quality.

And then there are the flaws built into collectors by the fact that they – and we – are human beings. We like to be praised, and the dealer who lauds our refined taste may be rewarded by a fat check. We are apt to rationalize paying for a piece we can't quite afford, telling ourselves that we'll just finance it by cutting back on Starbucks or putting off pedicures. We see buying and selling as a social interaction. We may purchase an antique chair to reward a dealer who has treated us kindly. Above all, we are vulnerable to the language of collecting, just as we are to the verbiage of politics. To some collectors, "rare" means good and "special" desirable – even though the speaker or writer may mean or know neither.

Language is powerful. We are swayed by rhetoric we do not correctly translate, and that is a weakness that can be and is preyed upon. In spending our collecting dollars, we are contortionists, behaving in manners contradictory to what we think of as deliberate and thoughtful. The irrational influences that shape our decisions are highlighted in a recently published book titled *Noise: A Flaw in Human Judgment*. While the authors focus primarily on professional decisions and their inconsistency, their ideas apply to the world of collecting – bluntly, how we spend our money.

The examples in *Noise* look at the professional worlds of law, medicine and the like and make one wonder how human beings ever make good decisions. For instance, judges give harsher sentences on days following their home football team's loss. Physicians are more likely to order cancer screenings for patients who they see early in the morning than those in late afternoon. Some social workers are much more likely to send children to foster homes than others (even if conditions are similar). The list goes on: seemingly whimsical decisions on bail, asylum, hiring, promotion. The theme of the book is this: "Whenever there is judgment there is noise – and more of it than you think." We live amidst distrac-

The Importance of the Word "Important"

tions, dislocations and misunderstood interactions, yet we must make decisions, sometimes swiftly, sometimes with incomplete information. Sound familiar, oh collector? It should.

When an issue of *Maine Antique Digest* (*MAD*) arrives, or *The Bee* or *The Magazine Antiques*, I am struck by the vibrancy of the current marketplace for American decorative arts and other genres. Money is being made. Attractive and interesting pieces are being discovered, researched, advertised, sold, rebought, and resold. Collectors are spending. I also am struck by something else. A good part of the marketplace's vitality revolves around the use of language, our very human noise. When it comes to buying and selling decisions, misused words can be as pernicious as the last-minute loss in a football scrum, or a patient seen in the afternoon.

As a retired college professor, I am steeped in notions endorsing the precise use of the written and spoken word, the power of language, the importance of being able to articulate one's ideas, positions, feelings, and observations. To paraphrase Joseph Conrad in *Lord Jim*, the power of the written word lies in its capacity to make the reader understand all that is before him – to hear, to feel, to see.

Language has a critical place in the antiques' market. It is used to help collectors feel, to see, understand, and – not incidentally – to buy. In one issue of *MAD* a dealer advertised a "rare and historically important" item. Another dealer's ad captioned a piece as "rare and important." And yes, yet a third dealer described an object as "rare and important." A fourth more modestly attached the tag "historically important" to an item. Struck by these repetitions, I took a look at the previous issue of *MAD*. Therein I found one "important," a "once in a lifetime," an extraordinary," an "exceptionally rare," and a "fabulous." I could go on, but you get the idea.

Hmmm, the psychologist in me said. What is the importance of <u>important</u>? What explains the proliferation of this adjective? Clearly, we are being wooed. Those wielding the word are trying to pique our interest while enhancing the perceived worth of the antique. Call it marketing, huckstering, or a dealer's heartfelt opinion. While I have no hard data, I think that the use of terms like <u>important </u>creates a noise that affects our decisions of what to buy and how much to pay. It is being used to im-

Lessons (Sometimes Waiting to Be Learned)

ply the antique is consequential, significant, momentous even, perhaps, historic. Just as the SOLD sign or red dot cause some collectors to pay attention to the good at hand, "important" may have the same effect: to make us pause, even to value the antique more highly.

Seasoned collectors most likely have learned not to grant adjectives or subjective valuations at face value. "Why is the piece important?" they ask instead. "How many pieces do you handle in a year that you feel are important?" "Aren't all antiques somehow important to someone at some time?" But such reasonable skepticism is not always at hand. Distraction, enthusiasm, and even environmental factors may work together with printed and verbal sales techniques to lead even the wisest of us astray, unconsciously.

"Important" is nothing more than a code word. There are many ways of communicating the idea without restoring to those particular nine letters. Some use words such as "extraordinary" or "fantastic." Or a piece may be described as "from the collection of a gentleman." If the owner has amassed a nice collection and a certain notoriety, "from the collection of _____ (fill in the name here)." We read of antiques that "descended in the family for several generations." Or ones that are "first time on the market in 80 years." Many ways exist to gain our attention and make a piece seem special. But carefully examined, the rhetoric seems to offer a good deal more than the substance might justify.

The "important," the "rare," the "unique," the "significant," the whatever are the salt on the boiled egg, the VSOP on the brandy bottle, the Baum and Mercier on the wristwatch. The terms also have the effect of suggesting the dealer or auction house is tasteful, established, exclusive and respectable, for that is why it permitted to buy and sell "important" antiques. The Halo Effect attached to important items lends other pieces in a dealer's inventory a new grace, deservedly or not.

Are collectors more satisfied if items in their collection that are thought to be important? Describing an antique as "important" is not just meant to satisfy a collector's need to own something marvelous, but to inspire the need itself. Yes, the word is noise. But it is also magic. "Important" is the bait, and the product is the hook.

Imagine a dealer has at hand a distinguished antique. Its attribution

The Importance of the Word "Important"

is well documented. We know what craftsmen made the desk in Philadelphia, to whom he sold it, and who had it in his possession as it descended in and moved out of the original owner's family. Provenance of this sort is crucial for some collectors. All these factors, taken together, justify the dealer assigning the label "important" to the piece. At other times, "important" is a synonym for "rare." If a craftsman made only a few clocks, sets of chairs of certain types, or tables, then each one is an important discovery.

Still, this chain of reasoning begs the question: Does the piece meet high standards of style and connoisseurship? In other word, it may be important, but is it any good? Its provenance may be important, but it still can be average in design, proportions, ornamentation, condition and a host of other ways.

What determines whether or not "important" is to be taken seriously is not the seller but the buyer. Collectors differ in what elements of style they value, so a piece could be desirable to one collector and not to another. Perhaps one collector is persuaded by the term "important" (that is, is unaware of the noise), and another is not. And the irrational does have a place in collecting. Affection for an item, its congruence with an existing collection, even the reminiscences it evokes can provide a rationale for purchasing.

"Important" should not be *verboten* for antiques collectors, though. I can readily understand museum displays using the term. Patrons and casual viewers come to be educated, to place what they are seeing within a material culture, historical period or movement. "I saw an important highboy at Colonial Williamsburg" they tell a friend. "It was a superb example of Chippendale style and someone who signed the Declaration of Independence owned it once." The significance of an object need not be minimized. At the same time, it should not be unjustifiably enhanced by the casual use of words.

We are back to where we started. Selling antiques and collecting them are part of a commercial enterprise in which information (text, images, history, provenance, condition, the object itself) is crucial. The business even has its own lingo, terms aptly foreign to those who are uninitiated. Among those terms are words, familiar to all, words that can confuse, hide and attract. "Buyer beware" is more than a cliché. It is the core rule of commerce. If we are beguiled by loose terminology, we may overlook cues pointing in other directions, alternative conclusions about the piece's attributes and desirability.

After all, isn't that when our education and knowledge are put to use . . . some would argue "best" put to use: Ignoring the hoopla and hype, deconstructing terms such as "extraordinary" or "important" and seeing the antique for what it truly is. We must labor to bring noise out of the closet, out of the shadows, into the full light of day, be fully conscious of what is influencing our decision to add a piece to our collection. Then if we decide to act irrationally, as we all do at times, it will be a matter of choice, not compulsion.

I walk through my collection and look at my country and high country furniture, a formal piece here and there, wooden work clocks, redware, homespun, and paintings. I believe that there is not an "important" piece in the entire assemblage (oh, maybe one). We have extensive knowledge of a few antiques we own – a painting of a schooner, a Roberts wooden work clock, a WWI British poster (*More Aeroplanes are Needed, Women Come and Help*), a Pan Am poster (*Across the Pacific in Five Days Via Pan America*; that's the possible important one). However, none of these may be objectively important. Yet my wife and I love dearly the individual pieces and the gestalt they create. Were any purchased because of noise? I do not know.

Of course, the wielding of language that sways and sells is only one of many forms of noise that influence collectors. We are moved to buy and admire because of talks by experts, wonderful color photographs, coffee table books highlighting noted collections, the reputations of dealers, shows and auction houses, and perhaps – yes – whether a collector is in a spending mood because his home football team won over the weekend. Welcome to collecting, to the spending of money, to the unknown influences that affect us.

Knowing that noise exists and may influence a collector's actions is an important(!) step in improving decision-making. It is one more tool that we all need to hone as collectors, not just because it is there and being used, but because we all want to collect wisely. Our forefathers knew the value of a good tool. We need to be like them.

Knowing about the various ways others try to influence collectors' purchases is critical to the hobby.

Chapter 25

The Prime Directive: Be Prepared

A seemingly unremarkable event got me thinking about a broader antique-collecting issue. For some reason, that happens. Maybe you react the same way. Recently I received an email from well-known dealers who were having a sale. The correspondence was nicely done – good photos, tempting prices. An Indian basket in two or three colors was one item listed. My wife and I had a place for one, but I never thought we needed just such a thing. We had not purchased that genre in many years. We already had two lidded Indian baskets, both showing vibrant colors and having no breaks (basket aficionados give primacy to the lack of such flaws in valuing the merits and aesthetics of these treasures). I looked at the price quoted by the dealers and my jaw dropped. Not only was the basket affordable, but it also seemed a bargain. That little revelation got me thinking about two things: (1) the market for American antiques and how it sets prices for Americana of all types and sizes, and the importance of collectors keeping abreast of market values for what we collect, and (2) the necessity of collectors knowing their own wants and tastes. Let's start with the market.

The global financial crisis of 2007-08 reordered the market for Americana. Except for the *crème de la crème* prices plummeted. As a collector I saw that when I attended shows, read *The Bee* and *Maine Antique Digest*, and purchased antiques. (As an aside – but an important one

The Prime Directive: Be Prepared

– it is difficult at times to judge the true value of an antique as reported in publications. It is not that the reporters and editors deliberately seek to deceive us. They simply do not want to bore readers and lack the print space that would be required to discuss each pictured or discussed item in depth – its condition, merits and flaws, style, attribution, and such.) The reformulation of prices for American antiques allowed my wife and me to upgrade our collection with items we never could have afforded at their pre-recession prices.

Still, a major question nags at the edge of my conscience. Have I been overpaying in the last decade when I thought I was getting a good deal? And what determined the price of the basket I bought and so enjoyed that I never dickered?

We have all heard the Economics 101 lecture, that supply and demand determine prices. The "market" is the power behind dollar signs. If there are only a few items of a particular sort or quality available for purchase and there are many eager and able buyers, the goods' prices increase. The obverse also is true. Ample supply coupled with weak demand leads to lower prices. In the case of American antiques (again excepting obviously superior and exceedingly rare pieces) the supply seems to have remained the same. It is collector demand that has diminished. For prices to stay at their earlier elevated levels, the stock of Americana would have to plummet, yet pieces kept entering the marketplace.

With disposable income for antiques (portfolio levels, dividends, monthly pensions, other interests such as vacations, college costs, and for a host of other reasons) in shorter supply following the last recession, collectors decided they still loved antiques but were not willing to pay what they had in the past to own them. Who can forget an auction prior to Antiques Week in Manchester, New Hampshire when one Queen Anne candle stand or table after another with nothing wrong with it was selling for under $200? The market was speaking loud and clear: Too much supply, not enough demand.

As you know, antique collectors do not formally get together to determine a list of "fair prices" for the items they seek. (Wouldn't such a convention of collectors be a hoot?) Instead, they influence the market one purchase (or lack of purchase), by one collector at a time. This demand affects the price of goods.

Dealers study the market closely. They analyzed the revaluation of items after the last sag in the antiques' market. Nothing has changed about the pieces themselves, except – and this is a critical "except" – the value buyers attached to them, the dollar amount we were willing to fork out to own (some might say rent) and enjoy them. Therefore, another force determining the cost of antiques, in response to and concert with collector's demand, is made up of a cadre of knowledgeable, influential dealers (and pickers) who pay attention to the market and have the data to show them what sells and what does not at various price points. This is not a simple task. As we all know, there are variables and factors that affect prices. It takes highly specialized (and frequently hard-won) knowledge to assess rarity, condition, provenance, the effect of where the item is for sale (auction venue, farmer's field) and other factors. I might note there are even evanescent issues of style and connoisseurship, something I address in Chapter 29.

Auction houses follow a path like that used by dealers in responding to lower demand in pricing items, and they also weighed in on the marketplace. When they work with consignors, they need an informed knowledge of the market, so items' reserves are fair enough to motivate bidders to wave their paddles and lead to the "going once, going twice, fair warning, sold" from the auctioneer, yet does not make the seller feel he has been lowballed. Even beautiful antiques go unsold if auctioneers (or consignors) misread the market or read it correctly for yesterday but incorrectly for today, and over-price the pieces for sale.

From a broad perspective the market for American antiques is pretty much a "free" one. Tariffs or tax structures do not exist to favor one mode of sales or one category of items over another. Auction houses and dealerships with varying pocketbooks and of different sizes compete on a relatively level playing field. No true monopolies exist. I suppose that the three or four eminent dealers specializing in the same genre could get together and seek to rig the market, but collectors always have the option and the power to do without and walk away. Attempts at an Americana oligopoly would not succeed. (Economists, learned folks in business, and politicians are concerned about the extent of limited competition, or oligopolies in our marketplaces. Do cell phone providers, airlines, and health insurance providers come to mind?)

It would be illuminating to talk with auctioneers and dealers as to how the falling prices played out over the years since 2007-2008 and if they are still playing out today. Were there terrible shows for dealers for months and months, or even years because of lowered demand in the face of their item pricing before they realized the market had re-ordered itself in a downward direction? Or did the old-timers know from previous economic downturns what was to come, and did they react almost instantly in lowering prices on their antiques for sale? Has the market stabilized – it has now been over a decade since our economic "collapse" or are the reverberations still being felt, collectors still deciding what a fair price is? I confess I do not know but I would lean to the latter. In any case, lower prices equal less profit unless dealers can turn over their wares more quickly and multiple times.

So, for a variety of reasons at the "macro" level a new market has been established for American antiques, and I, one collector (surely the micro level) find myself making sense of and adjusting to it. We are back to the Indian basket I recently purchased. I mentioned I did not haggle over price. I did not want to seem pushy to the dealers. (Knowing the market prevents collectors from acting like arses beating up a dealer over price.) I was so pleased by the listed price (as compared in my head to what our baskets cost years ago) I was stunned. The price seemed equitable. But to tell the truth, I should have taken a few minutes to look at the market for baskets. After all, that is one of the prime directives to any collector – know the market in which you are buying so as to not overpay, to perhaps get a really good deal, and to spend your limited dollars wisely. Did I overpay? No, once I investigated the market for Indian painted baskets the price was fair. I concluded it is a great time to build a collection of painted American (toss in Canadian) baskets. Have I been overpaying for other pieces in the last decade? I hope not as I have, to the best of my abilities kept abreast of and knew their market costs.

Nonetheless, a problem still exists for collectors (myself included). I am up to speed on baskets but what about other genres that I might encounter at a show? If I know what I will be looking for (fair disclosure – redware with writing on it, for example) I have kept up on the market and researched it. No problem there. But what about categories and their prices I used to know well but for one reason or another (no place for one, thought my taste had moved on, have not seen an example worth looking at in years, etc.) I now am uncertain of. What about a piece in a genre I know little about that simply "speaks to me?" Hmmm. I have no ready solutions. (If one is listed on a dealer's website or at auction, I often have time to assess the market.) At a show – I could put a hold on it and then sit in a corner with my smart phone and look at dealers' websites or auction house results but really . . .? My advice would be to talk with the dealer, especially if you are familiar with her or have heard good things about her and see what she has to say. Of course, you can bargain but you may not know if the starting price is too high (in your estimation once you learn more). I confess that I have no sure-fire solutions.

I have less to say on the second issue before us, but by no means intend to give it short shrift. It simply seems more opaque, more difficult to get a handle on, despite its central importance for any collector. It is time to look at another surprise when the basket knocked on my door – a collector's tastes and wants. But if collectors know anything, I hear you state, they know what they like and want. *Au contraire*, I respond, the basket being a case in point. Obviously, my wife and I like such baskets. We have lived for many years with two nice examples. But if you had asked me, I would have told you my tastes had changed, that we owned as many baskets as we needed and wanted, that baskets were not on the list of what antiques I sought. I was wrong, and that error gave me pause. How does a collector know his own tastes? The question as I pose it sounds kind of inane, but it is not meant to be so.

One way forward to an answer is to take money out of the collecting equation. Ask yourself the questions, Would I be interested in another weathervane, tall case clock or tavern table (or whatever is in your collection) if it was free? What attributes would the piece need? The basket was so inexpensive (to me) that purchasing it did not prevent me from seeking other pieces. In that sense it was "free." Or put money back in the equation. Ask yourself questions such as Would I be interested in a superb example of an antique at a fair price? What ads grab my attention, what items in booths or pictured on dealer or auction websites do I gravitate toward? What is on my mental list to consider purchasing? What in my collection do I want to upgrade? Have some fun walking through and look at your collection, really look at it, and ask yourself these questions. You may be startled at the answers. You will certainly learn something about the current state of affairs of what you covet. Or you may be completely surprised, as I was, when a proverbial basket whispers in your ear, a discovery of a previous much-loved genre.

The trope, *caveat emptor*, let the buyer beware, is one worth heeding, emotionally if for no other reason. I would have been disappointed but not devastated had I overpaid for the basket by a bit, since it was (to me) inexpensive, and my comparison price-point involved baskets purchased many years ago and costing hundreds of dollars more. I would have remonstrated myself to be more prepared, the purpose and major theme of this column, but would not have fallen on my sword. Of course, if the item in question had cost me many thousands of dollars, and I could have saved thousands by knowing the marketplace please get my sword so I can fall on it. The matter of my tastes was answered immediately. I liked the way the basket looked. It appealed to me emotionally.

My advice to seasoned collectors is this: Be careful my friends. Prices have somewhat adjusted to the world economic crisis of a decade ago, but it is our responsibility to know and adjust to the current marketplace. And do not discount supply and demand. When I began collecting redware with writing they were commonly for sale. Since then, they are few and far between. Some examples are much less costly now, some are not. Knowledge of the marketplace for them is important. The best of any genre seldom enters the marketplace and is to be treasured. Collectors expect to pay high prices for the best. But a collector still needs to know the market for the best, as well as the rest of what we collect.

And for self-knowledge, our tastes and wants, as compared with knowing the market, the former is the more difficult as one would expect of any form of knowing oneself. What are we seeking? Both forms of preparation I have discussed (market and ourselves) aid and assist a seasoned eye and allow great antiques to grab you by the collar and drag you

Lessons (Sometimes Waiting to be Learned)

to them (now there's an image for you). It was my basket purchase that drove home the reality that such knowledge is an ongoing process. Why would I have expected otherwise? Being prepared is easier said than done but collectors who have done their homework often reap the benefit. The Roman Seneca's famous quote is apt: "Luck is a matter of preparation meeting opportunity." Prepare and then go forth in your hunt for antiques. And good luck.

Collectors spend a lifetime being prepared. They can never be too attuned to the market, have too much knowledge, or have too good an eye.

Chapter 26

Surrounded by One's Collection or Not

I collect Americana, and I live with my collection. I sit on Windsor chairs crafted long ago, have lamps on antique tables, hang artwork that limners painted, use firkins for wastebaskets, snuggle under homespun blankets, and count on draft-fighting wingback chairs to fend off Wisconsin's winter nights. But if you told me I would have to store my collection out of sight, bringing it out only when I wanted to enjoy it, I would not be a collector of Americana.

Someone who collects stamps has them in albums or mounted or stored in other ways, and they are out of sight most of the time, too precious to handle. A coin collector has his coins in albums or sleeves, not to be tarnished by an ungloved hand ever again, squirreled away. In the same vein, a collector I know of America's past is married to an unimpressed wife in that his collection resides in drawers or in binders inside bookcases or cabinets. He collects everything paper – ephemera if you will – related to the state in which he lives: historic letters, contracts, postcards, and such. His wife finds his collecting in this manner "totally bizarre." He told me that "She can understand the desire for the item, but how could the item be so important to the collector if it is hidden away from view where it may only be seen once a year or even less frequently?" She raises a very good question indeed, but responsibility, knowledge, commitment, and mission surely nourish her collecting spouse, even if he must open chests and closets to look at his collection.

I admit I collected stamps as a boy and teen, but I would not collect them now. Evidently something changed within me. I know stamps can be beautiful works of art, and their attraction to those who collect them is as strong as my lust for certain American antiques. But as I age, fulfilling my aesthetic needs becomes more compelling. I want to be surrounded by pieces that enlighten and delight me, not by ones that must be pampered, concealed, fretted about, and occasionally pulled into daylight. What is the *raison d'etre* of being a collector who lives amidst his collection and uses and can see it, and another who stows it away? Let's take a look.

Collectors who live with their collections daily and those who put them away share many similarities – the thrill of The Hunt, euphoria at a great find, a love of history, documenting their items, an appreciation for the beautiful (even if the beautiful is barbed wire), a desire for the rare, and so forth. Hobbies add an extra dimension to collectors' lives, regardless of what they covet and collect. All collectors may be victimized by rumors, fads and bubbles that say what is now "in" and desirable. Collectors of all shapes and forms make up communities, now readily connected by the internet and handy devices. Serious collectors are pleased to find fellow collectors with whom to share their commitment and accomplishments. whether in person, via publications, or penned letters to the editor of a favorite publication that is a must read given what they collect. There exist many ways to let the world know about their tastes, successes and assembled pieces.

Novice collectors of stamps and coins have holes to fill – literally. A Scott's stamp album or blue Whitman coin holder has spaces for each stamp or coin in a series. Of course, a more experienced collector would leave some of those "holes" empty, only buying the best he could afford. For others the holes are metaphorical. A collector of comic books, matchbooks, saltshakers or whatever undoubtedly knows what is crucial to having a complete series, a grouping representative of a certain era, a style, or material. The wealthy solon who collects antique cars may sneer at a Rolls Royce because he only desires Duesenbergs (these collections are a bit harder to hide, admittedly, but we regularly are amused by suddenly discovered "barn finds," so it is certain some collectors of these hulking beauties keep them for their own private pleasure). So, really, it appears that few differences exist between types of collectors.

Condition is another variable on which differences are difficult to find. A coin collector will upgrade, sometimes at great cost, the condition of a coin he already owns, just as a collector of redware or painted boxes might. To all of us – all things being equal and unless an item is so rare as to be almost unique – condition is a holy grail. But fingerprints on a Louis XIV armoire will hardly affect its value, while those on a mint $50 gold piece would materially affect its rarity and monetary worth. At the same time, the number of such *rara avis* pieces is infinitesimally tiny and incomprehensibly costly. Most of us have neither the fortune nor the curse to live with such items.

One difference between how collections are displayed or stored may be the need to encounter one's treasures. As someone who lives with his American antiques, I see them daily and I am reminded, if I pay attention to them (an important if), of their beauty and the stories that lay behind each piece. One would think that unless a stamp, coin or comic book collector takes part of his collection out each night to look at and pore over it, the need to see and be reminded is weaker, to enjoy it regularly is weaker than it is for a collector such as myself. That notion would be incorrect. In talking to such collectors, one learns that they can call up in their mind's eye individual stamps, coins, or other pieces, remember the stories behind them, and enjoy them as fully as someone who lives surrounded by the objects he collects. And those of us whose collections are in plain sight become hardened to them over time because they are so familiar, sometimes not noticing the pieces we once so yearned for. Appreciation – like affection – is a sensitive, conscious act.

One collector with whom I spoke said his comic book collection, quite good, was put together when he was much younger, and the items much less expensive. His joy in his collection – he is not active now – is based in nostalgia for his youth. He is also aware that committing too much time to his comic books might rekindle his desire to collect again, and to avoid the temptation to spend yet more on them, he not only limits the time he spends with his own youthful, colorful treasures but avoids stores that sell comic books as well. He considers himself a lapsed collector. Faced with the same dilemma, a collector of Americana would not simply box up her treasures but sell them.

One difference between those who live with the past and those who sock it away may be that the latter have a greater need for distance, objectivity and contemplation than those of us whose collections gather dust in plain sight. I seldom sit quietly and study pieces in my American antique collection. If I had to dig it out, looking at what I have would be a break from the daily humdrum, a special moment. My consolation is that I live inside my collection. I am both with and in America's history, craftsmanship and taste. That is a powerful motivator and an even more powerful reminder.

Search as I might and tempting as it may be, I could find no data substantiating the stereotype of the stamp or coin collector as an introvert, most comfortable with pieces of paper or metal, preoccupied with minute details, magnifying glass and fountain pen in hand. Heck, even collectors of large pieces of furniture or artwork are as preoccupied with particulars as are most who indulge in stamps, coins or barbed wire. The cliché would have it that those who pursue exotica like "bob-whar" (as a colleague pronounces it) are strange. All I can say is that the collecting mania, no matter the subject, is weird – not in a scary sense, mind you, but just foreign to those who are not infected with it. So many people collect so many types of things that to think of certain collectors as eccentric begs the issue of what is normal.

One difference between those who live with what they collect and those who stow it away is that collectors like me, who confront their collections every day, come face to face with their mistakes. The feeling I have blundered does not wane with time, I hate to say. For those whose collections are out of sight, separation exists between their daily and collecting lives. The stimuli for remembering such errors in collecting judgment are stowed away. While they can remember their gems and triumphs, the proverb "out of sight, out of mind" typically prevails. There is no omnipresent reminder of those painful moments of blundering until they haul their collection out. I envy that at times but being surrounded by history largely makes up for it.

Surrounded by One's Collection or Not

For many genres there is a clear difference between the visible and "invisible" collections. The distinction refers to where items are found and how unexpected their discovery is. For American antiques one still hears about great finds in antique malls, junk stores, flea markets, or house sales. People simply may not know when that chair or table was made, its pedigree and what it is worth. The same is true for some Asian items, when the $35 bowl becomes a six-figure windfall. In stark contrast stand coins, stamps, comic books, really ancient texts, fine art and a host of other desirables. For coins, the unexpected discovery rarely happens, nor does it for stamps or comic books. The values of these pieces have been nearly standardized: a coin of a certain vintage and certified condition can be had for X dollars. A few taps on the keys of a cellular phone reveals what the piece should cost. That is hardly the case for items such as matchbook covers and other ephemera, that crop up unexpectedly and attain unexpected values, both of which can add to the fun.

To be clear, collectors do not choose the genre with which they fall in love and covet based on whether their collection will surround them or not. Perhaps a parent or other family member motivated their interest in the genre, or a spouse, a protagonist in a novel, a friend? For whatever reason, the collecting flame was lit, and the collector thinks little of the fact his stamps go into albums, or that the artwork is hung on walls. For if you are a collector on a mission, you are left with few choices as to how your collection is cared for. In that sense you are merely at the service of what you love. It does not matter that your pieces are put away. You feel no loss at this. You have more important goals than to be surrounded by what you are collecting.

A practical difference between types of collections is the issue of providing security. A collection that is portable is easily stolen, compared with furniture and heavy, bulky objects. What do stamp or coin collectors do to "secure" their collections – safes, hidden rooms, under lock and key? Improved home security is a must, and many alternatives exist in the age of smart phones and the internet. A safety deposit box offers maximum security, but such a collection is not easily accessible for viewing or to share with others. Depending on the collection's value, the collector may have little choice. Even I, with beds and chairs and benches concede the need for a good home alarm system, since I cannot use a safe. In effect, my dwelling is my safe.

When I set out to write on this topic, I expected to find marked differences between collectors of different genres but did not. For while the collector's wife I referred to at the beginning of this piece may not understand her husband's passion for items stored in drawers and closets, handling them in this manner makes perfect sense. Where a collection resides is secondary. What is critical is that the collecting game remains afoot. The objects become almost incidental at times to The Hunt, the lust, the passion, and the need to learn, preserve and share. For whether a collection is lived with or stashed, it becomes an extension of a serious collector – an important, valuable extension.

I am old fashioned and still pay many bills by US mail. When I go to the post office, I am struck by how beautiful some of the new issues of stamps are and I remember why I collected stamps as a boy and teen. But the twists and turns that make up anyone's life put me on an Americana path. Were my life different, I would be taking out my stamp collection as soon as this essay is completed to enjoy it, while plotting and mapping out what stamp or series I should pursue next.

Some collectors' pieces lie in plain sight, for others they are put away. What we love to collect determines this.

Chapter 27

The Three Ghosts of Purchasing Antiques

Ebenezer was sound asleep, or had been, or thought he was. He opened one eye and saw what looked very much like a ghost. "Can't be," he said and lay back down. But the noise: groaning and chains clanking. One heck of a dream, he thought to himself.

"Ebenezer, wake up," the voice repeating itself, getting louder. Ebenezer sat up in bed and looked around, both eyes wide open now.

"Who or what are you?" Ebenezer asked.

"I am the Ghost of Buyer's Remorse," the spirit groaned. "There are lessons for you to learn tonight. I am the first of three ghosts that will visit you." He thrust a trembling finger at Eb.

Ebenezer shook his head. "I know of Dickens and *A Christmas Carol*. Truth be told, I am scared out of my mind, never having been visited by apparitions before. Why me; what did I do to deserve this? Oh, how I wish for the brightness of a new day."

"You are everyman," the ghost roared, "every collector who has bought and built a collection. And when the night is finished, you will have lessons to teach them all." The ghost was persuasive, that's for sure.

"You said you were the Ghost of Buyer's Remorse," Ebenezer replied. "But I love my collection and the treasured objects within it. They make me smile."

Lessons (Sometimes Waiting to be Learned)

"Do not fool with me," the ghost replied. He was becoming upset. "That portrait you purchased last year, how unhappy you are with it. Oh, you told yourself you were tired and that is why you did not look closely enough at it. You talked yourself into buying the piece. You wanted to leave the show with something. But once you got it home (the ghost swept his arm across Ebenezer's bedroom) it didn't look the way you envisioned. Then there was the painted Pennsylvania blanket chest you had to own because your good friend Fred has one and you decided you always liked it. Until you owned one like it, that is." The ghost was becoming impatient, his voice rising, scaring Ebenezer even more. "Actually, it was better off with Fred. But still you tossed and turned many a night because of your mistakes."

"But all collectors make such mistakes," Ebenezer replied.

"Then why does it bother you so?" asked the ghost. "Are you so perfect as to not make them? Need I give you a list of your buyer's mistakes? Let's see, there was the fancy fridge, the iridescent polo shirt, the newfangled lightbulbs. At least you like your home, unlike some I have visited who regret that enormous purchase."

"Am I not allowed to be imperfect in my taste and decision making?" Ebenezer replied. "American antiques have a host of criteria that makes them good or better or best. Am I to master them all? No collector wants to tell himself, 'I blew it.' Even Henry Ford, a noted collector of Americana is quoted as saying in the book American Treasure Hunt, '. . . I'm greatly disappointed in having been fooled.' But it happens."

Ebenezer had said his piece.

"I know it happens," spat the Ghost of Buyer's Remorse. "I know the feeling of regret when faced with two or three choices – look at all the weathervanes – choosing one and later, or not so later, knowing you should have picked another, or none. And I know you work hard for your antique dollars, making the regret even more profound."

"Then why are you here? "Ebenezer repeated.

"I am here because you did not research the painting sufficiently," the ghost murmured. "I am here because you blamed others and did not learn from your choices, yours alone. It was not the dealer that pressured you or auction fever." By this time the ghost was roaring loudly. "This is not a case of your auto being recalled for a defect you could not have known of. I am here because you were unprepared and asked too few questions. I am here to give you an ethereal kick in the pants."

Ebenezer sighed. "If you are going to teach me lessons for the future, what are they?"

"You could have waited, trusted yourself and your eye. Had you done so, the painting and blanket chest you then purchased would have added to your collection as you had hoped."

"But I felt I was prepared," Ebenezer said in his own defense. "I liked the blanket chest when I purchased it. I loved it, desired it, wanted it. It was full of heightened possibilities." Eb swung his arm to encompass the bedroom the way the ghost had.

"All well and good," said the ghost. "But you make too many mistakes."

"Yes," said Ebenezer, "I could have been better prepared, to be more selective. I am angry about the 'opportunity costs' of the purchases. A painting I truly loved entered the market, and at a lower price, soon after I purchased this one, but alas, I had no funds."

The ghost smiled. "You are showing a bit of humility and insight. I like that. And the piece of mochaware you have been seeking for years, look at Sotheby's auction catalog, you will see it listed, but now you have no antique dollars left to spend."

At this news Eb groaned. "What do you think of the painting?" he asked the ghost.

"I feel the same way about it your collector friends do," the ghost replied. "It doesn't quite seem to fit into your collection, nor is it up to your usual standards. Where I come from one might wonder why in the hell you bought it at all?"

Ebenezer had never quite had a night like this one. He attempted to banish the Ghost of Buyer's Remorse using psychological gyrations. "I know, the painting isn't perfect or what I hoped for, but it is 'okay.'"

"Don't go reducing your dissonance as a way of making me feel better," the ghost roared again. "And no games about how little effort it took to find it. You and I both know you put in a great deal of effort, but the purchase still went awry. Okay isn't good enough."

"But I have options," Ebenezer whined. "I can hide the painting away or live with it or sell it. I'd lose some money but still replenish my antiques' account. Better than nothing."

"Well, everyman," the ghost said. His chains were getting heavy, and he looked tired himself. "As a collector you must learn from your mistakes when purchasing antiques. If you do so you will become more astute. And you will sleep better, and I shall leave you alone. But you will be visited by two more ghosts tonight." And the ghost smiled sardonically and vanished.

Ebenezer sighed. One heck of a dream. It all seemed so realistic. And in his own way he was curious. And he fell back asleep. Only to be awakened moments later by yet another ghost.

"And who are you?" Ebenezer asked.

"I am the Ghost of Slim Pickings," the specter announced, grimacing.

"Sounds like a country and western singer ," Ebenezer retorted.

"Do you mock me, sir?" asked the ghost, filling the room with his persona, not a pleasant sight at all.

Ebenezer stayed silent. It seemed like the proper and judicious thing to do.

"Remember a few months ago when you experienced a 'drought'?" the ghost said. Oh, you kept abreast of the antiques in the marketplace but nothing that interested you appeared. How you gnashed your teeth and suffered so."

"It was a terrible time," Ebenezer agreed. "I had not yet purchased the painting or blanket chest. I had dollars galore and nothing to buy with them."

"And you call yourself a collector," the ghost smirked. "You should appreciate the rhythm, the ebb and flow of antiques being available. But in droughts there are no goods to even lean toward buying. And you couldn't wait," the ghost roared.

"I forgot about that," Ebenezer whispered. And the more he whispered the louder the ghost's voice became.

"You forgot! Bah, sir. How could you forget not being able to bid at the auction for the table you wanted so? And the show last month when you rushed toward the piece of silver only to realize you were broke. You forgot? I think not."

Ebenezer said nothing. He thought to himself, that is why I bought the painting. I was so frustrated I forgot that all droughts come to an end. And it cost me dearly.

"Yes!" said the ghost. "And now, not to be cruel . . ."

"But you seem to enjoy being cruel," Ebenezer interrupted.

"Aye, I do sometimes." And the ghost smiled. "But how else will you learn your lesson? Droughts typically end in a downpour of desired antiques that collectors covet. You could not suffer the pain of waiting." And the ghost slowly faded into the ectoplasmic distance.

"Whew," said Ebenezer. "I'll never forget those lessons again."

"But they are not the worst." A third ghost had filled the room, his voice booming and reverberating.

"Not the worst?" stammered Ebenezer.

"Not even close. Remember the show where the antique of your dreams was before you. I do not see it in your collection," the third shade chided. "A few years ago, you thought the Dutch candlesticks were too expensive, only in retrospect changing your mind, and by then it was too late. The worst agony a collector experiences is when he does not buy a piece he could and should have. I am the Ghost of 'Non-Buyer's Remorse.'"

Ebenezer pulled the covers over his head to protect himself from the pain. For the ghost was correct.

"Now, Ebenezer," said the spirit, "in the next 20 seconds I want you to name three antiques you should have bought but did not. The clock is ticking."

Ebenezer did not even have to think for a moment. "The yellow Shaker yellow box, the early 19th century needlepoint, and the wonderful tallcase clock."

"You blew it," said the ghost.

"Yes," Ebenezer said. "I have rued those decisions for months – no years – and they haunt me to this very evening. I can see them still as plainly as I can see you, and they trouble me equally so." A few tears trickled down his face. "I loved them so."

The ghost smiled. "You had the opportunity and did not pull the trigger. You had the fiscal wherewithal."

"I should have bought them," Ebenezer whispered. "I failed," and he whispered even more softly, "and I know I failed."

"That is why the pain is so acute," the ghost said.

"I was an idiot to let those pieces go to someone else," Ebenezer said. "Difficult to rationalize away that self-knowledge, that aggravation at oneself." The ghost towered over Ebenezer, but he was smiling. His lesson seemed to be seeping in.

"You forgot, didn't you? Buy something that 'pops'; look for a piece that is quite good, regardless of the genre. If you love it, buy it!"

It had been a long night and Ebenezer sighed deeply. "It is not the ones that got away that are so memorable or painful, it is the ones I let get away that trouble me so. Those pieces were perfection, and I could have bathed in perfection's bliss."

"Everyone experiences non-buyer's remorse," the ghost replied. "It is so common that there even exists a website for clothes shoppers, The One That Got Away, so that sorrowing fashionistas can be reunited with the beloved clothing item they carelessly passed over."

"Oh, how I wish such a website existed in the American antique community! I will do better, I promise," Ebenezer said. And then he heard the faint peal of the morning bell.

When Ebenezer awoke, he threw open his bedroom window. No prize turkey to buy despite the holiday season. But he felt he was a better collector. Was it all a dream?

It is probably a given, that I have omitted some ghosts that visit you but did not visit Ebenezer. Those who do not collect may be perplexed as to why Ebenezer put up with the ghosts' visits. But the scary nights are the price a collector pays for the pleasures and satisfactions collecting brings. Ebenezer, like most collectors must endure the irritations buying sometimes brings, hopefully with grace and aplomb, in this case with quite an evening.

In fact, all collectors have heard Ebenezer's ghosts rattle their chains in the dark hours of the night. And a happy holiday to you all.

Collectors purchase with high spirits and haunting ones.

Sleep well.

Chapter 28
A Timed Auction

Lot 273 intones the auctioneer. You really like the water, sailboats and view of West Point, a Hudson Valley painting. Thirty seconds later it is either yours or a competitor's. The auctioneer has already moved on to Lot 274. All your due diligence, lusting, fantasy of hanging the work on a perfect place at home for it, is over before you can take but a few breaths. That is auctions as we used to know them. Then, timing was everything. Today collectors may face an entirely different phenomenon, the so-called timed auction.

There is a certain irony in the terminology, for the new auction strategy (It may have been tried earlier in the antiques world, but my recollection goes back to the Manchester Show in 2020) stretches time, makes it indefinite. Instead of auctioning off items one after the other – partly on the Internet but also with some in-person bidders – timed auctions extend for a number of days. When they close, there is typically a grace period. if someone bests a collector's bid for an item, the auction is extended for a period, say 15 minutes. That way no one can bid with five seconds remaining and claim the piece.

That certainly differs from the customary antique auction, although eBay sellers (eBay began in 1995) have been holding timed auctions for years, the only difference being that the on-line site offers a "buy it now" feature, where for a given price, the item is yours. As an aside it is not

Lessons (Sometimes Waiting to be Learned)

uncommon for eBay offerings sell for more than their "buy it now" price. The bidding is wide-open and, as we all know, lust sometimes trumps common sense.

The initiation of timed auctions in antique dealings hearkens one of those revolutions that crop up now and then. I have already used the term "strategy" in reference to this particular innovation, and where strategy raises its head, the psychologist wants to get into it, which is precisely what I intend to do. What is the psychology of a timed auction? How is a bidder to proceed, and what governs bidding and winning?

Collectors bidding at timed auctions need strategies and they need to know their inclinations. For some, the goal is paying the least possible amount for a desired antique. For others, the goal is to have fun, and if that requires paying a bit more, so be it. Some collectors bid exclusively in the last few minutes. Others, just like in poker, enjoy the tension of bidding, having one's bid raised by someone else, and the back and forth, perhaps over the course of days, as the money in the pot climbs. A timed auction allows days to rationalize, obsess, fall in love, be honest with or delude yourself. But there are some ways to increase the chances of winning the item you want, and at a fair price, if that is your goal.

As is typical at old-fashioned in-person auctions, "ask and you shall receive" is an illusion. Oftentimes items bring a higher price if they bear a lower reserve and the starting bid makes the item seem more affordable. Additionally, more people can become involved in the bidding on that particular piece and can follow it over the days of the auction. In other words, the idea of "anchoring" – that collectors will adjust if a higher price sets a challenge – does not work in the real world of timed auctions.

What does a lower reserve do besides attracting more collectors' attention? At a timed auction it allows more bidders to become emotionally involved with a piece. You would think that since a timed auction lacks the frenzy – the last few minutes notwithstanding – of a regular auction, bidders could make rational decisions on how much to bid and whether to continue bidding. You would be wrong. Yes, bidders have time to look at their checkbooks, think about the cost, talk with others, and make a deliberate decision. But they also have time for their emotions to weigh on them – how much they love the piece, the fantasies of the antique

A Timed Auction

placed in their home, and the like. Bidders, just as at auctions that take place in real time, may inadvertently develop a sense of ownership for particular pieces, driving prices higher. Despite the fact that timed auctions are perfectly designed to allow bidders to arrive at rational decisions, oftentimes they do not.

We now have insight into why bidders might bid in the early moments of a timed auction. Some collectors like to get their oar in the water and hope that no one else will want to set sail. The outcome: a hoped-for great bargain. Although that may occur once in a while, other reasons exist for early bidding. After all, bidders know that most of the time if they bid early, they cannot possibly be the only person who has noticed and wants the piece and that more bids will be placed. But the experience of fun, competition, tension, and involvement can all supersede the rationality of getting the antique at the best possible price.

Merely because a collector cannot see or hear others in the auction room does not diminish a sense of competition, so it is as prevalent in timed auctions as it is in conventional ones. Gore Vidal probably said it best (although not referring to auctions per se): "It is not enough to succeed, others must fail." Bidding early communicates to every other bidder on that item that they have an opponent. Yes, outbidding others early on may eliminate some potential competitors. On the other hand, outbidding others with days left gives them lots of time to respond with an even higher bid. Showing other bidders that you mean business by raising the bids within minutes of their bidding (except near the end of the auction) may increase a sense of excitement, produce auction fever and competitiveness, and have the opposite effect (unanticipated outcome) that you hoped for. Instead of scaring them off, you hook them in.

Emotions and irrationality enter into a timed in another way. Bidders may experience the "rose-colored-glasses effect." As you think about (feel about) an item you may find yourself focusing on its positive attributes, overlooking its faults that prevent it from being a "nine" or "ten." As you look at the item over the days in a timed auction, the positive attributes can grow larger, the negatives diminish. At least that is your perception.

Obviously, but it bears repeating, bidding at timed auctions last far longer than a typical auction with which collectors of American antiques are more familiar. The research shows the more time a bidder spends attending to an item, the more he is willing to pay. Collectors (bidders) at a timed auction may become psychologically trapped. They cannot bring themselves to give the item up.

I found one piece of especially interesting advice. If your goal is to win the piece, do not bid early in a timed auction. Auction houses and consignors like early bidding because it creates buzz – it is likely to create interest in that antique and sends up a flare, drawing others' attention to it. I know this to be true from my own experiences. When I look at a timed auction and return the next day or two, and another day or two after that, I find myself drawn to items that already have several bids. I find myself thinking that the piece in question must be a good one because it already has drawn the attention of others. Other bids are seducing me. They are offering "social proof" the item is good, desirable, perhaps rare. So, the best way to bid, apparently, to maximize your chances of winning, is to wait. Wait until near the end of a timed auction. See what the leading bid is, and then enter your own. In other words, cut it close.

An odd downside to bidding early is that you may win a piece that is interesting, but not compelling, at a price that once seemed prudent and now seems excessive. You are obligated to buy it. And in the days remaining on a timed auction other pieces may have become available elsewhere. Or you may have looked more closely at other items in the same auction and decided you like (love) one of these more. Give yourself time. Be deliberate.

I recently viewed a timed online auction with three hours left. Forty-one of 331 pieces (12.4%) had bids on or above their high estimate and 12 of those were for stoneware or redware (was that because of conservative estimates, or was it the result of high demand?). Only a handful of pieces had no bids at all. At a second timed auction (same auction house) held at the same time, 104 of 620 offerings (16.7%) had a bid at or above the high estimate with three hours remaining. Seventy-eight pieces (12.6%) had no bids. So, most collectors are bidding well before the end of the auction.

Should you bid at the lowest price possible or try to shut out the competition and bid at a level above (perhaps far above) the minimum to "shut down" competitors. Experienced bidders tell me to put in a higher bid, rather than a smaller one. Doing so eliminates "nibbling bidders" (bargain hunters) and reduces the competition for the item. Show that you mean business. Of course, unless you absolutely love the piece your high bid should not be above market value, but if you have to own it, it can be. Other serious buyers may be lurking. You probably do not want to bid your maximum right away (assuming you can stick to that maximum bid anyway). And, as is true of any auction, if the item truly exceeds your budget, stop! Easier said than done. Some experts even advise to bid only once. In any case, bid the maximum you are willing to pay for the antique and if someone bests your bid, withdraw.

You may already have discovered the real essence of a timed auction. The only true bidding occurs in the last few minutes, when serious bidders wholeheartedly dive in with the dollars they are willing to pay. That is when auction fever may be at its highest, emotions overrule what your head has decided, and the devil actually is in the details, sometimes known as decimal points. That is the moment serious buyers cherish and remember.

Timed auctions online use software that automatically informs a bidder when she has been outbid. Often a statement accompanies such a message, "It's almost yours!" or "You can increase your chances of winning this item if you increase your bid," accompanied by a button you only need click to bid once more. Process such messages as rationally as you can. You may well know you have funds available, and the item has not reached your limit. Wait – what is the hurry? Think about it. Do not respond immediately.

A basic piece of advice: If you are going to bid near the end of a timed auction, make sure you are logged in to the auction with enough time to settle yourself and make good decisions. Nothing impairs decision making like having trouble gaining access to the auction and doing so with only minutes to spare. Avoid that anxiety-inducing experience. Also, it is not unusual for a collector to be bidding on more than one item at a timed auction online. If you are bidding on multiple items, you will need time to set up your screens typically with a different auction page on each so you can easily follow multiple items.

Lessons (Sometimes Waiting to be Learned)

But for goodness sakes, be careful and avoid accidental bids, called "mis-clicks." These are not a problem in a live online auction (except perhaps in the case of an extremely difficult auctioneer) and are immediately correctable. But with many individuals bidding in the last moments, they are becoming more common (truth be told, they can also occur earlier in an online timed auction, but the bid usually can be cancelled). Now that so many auctions are online, it's a bit of a problem, and one that is exacerbated with the throngs of people who take part in last-second bidding.

Lot 273. Someone bids in the last 10 minutes extending the timed auction. You bid again and wait, anguish in the waiting. Finally, the lot is yours. Let's hope the pandemic ends and the "new normal" of auctions ends with it. But some auction houses are choosing to keep timed affairs seeing this as an exciting alterative to the man-behind-the-podium.

In timed auctions, often he who hesitates is saved.

Chapter 29

Using Style and Connoisseurship Criteria to Buy the Best We Can Afford

I was late to the party, figuratively. For years I had wondered about a question to which I found no answer. The question: What does a collector do when his eye exceeds his budget? After all, a collector is repeatedly urged to train his eye. We are commanded to look at a variety of forms and surfaces in a genre and then look at more. That is why Albert Sack's book known as *Good, Better, Best* is so valuable. In his book we can put three versions of the same table, chest, or clock side by side and compare them, one with the other. We can do the same in dealer's shops shows and auctions. And after a time, if we are diligent and observant, we begin to learn what makes a particular piece desirable, at least to us.

After many years I had trained my eye, in the parlance of today. I had refined and deepened my sense of style, even become a bit of a connoisseur. I didn't know then that there existed clearly delineated criteria for assessing a piece of Americana, yet I did know what I liked and why. At the same time, I did know that antiques were for sale that I lusted after but were often beyond my financial means. I could not afford the pieces I knew were the best. A friend was kind enough to offer me the consolation of Robert Browning: "Ah, but a man's reach should exceed his grasp, / Or what's a heaven for?" Aspiration, ambition, ideals are deeply human

Lessons (Sometimes Waiting to be Learned)

traits, and indeed we should revel in being human to the extent we chase perfection. That said, I was still frustrated. How, I wondered, was I to deal with this dilemma . . . a conundrum faced by every collector – well, almost every – at one time or another?

Let me propose that in any genre of Americana it is usually agreed that certain forms are ideal. These are the *10s*, beautiful to behold, expensive to purchase. By definition they are almost always beyond the means of the general run of collectors. When certain antique toys sell for over $100,000, paintings for seven figures, Windsor chairs for tens of thousands the air gets thin at the top of the American antiques' marketplace. Fortunate indeed is the rare collector for whom the best-of-the-best is affordable, and even for her an object might sometimes be a painful stretch.

Lately, as I have mentioned, my attention has turned to collecting redware plates and platters with names or writing on them. I did not do so because such redware was within my means but out of passion, yet it turns out for example that a fabulous "ABC" plate at auction from a well-known collection was affordable. I still fantasize about coming across a redware platter made when Lafayette visited in the United States with the names "Washington" and "Lafayette" in slip. Could I afford it? It depends. How many other redware collectors and dealers would also covet such a treasure? How deep would I be willing to reach to own it? And it depends on is condition. Still, it might be possible. My point is simply this: Collectors are only limited by taste and connoisseurship. Beyond that point we have to be reasonable, to assess our capacity and limits, and to be knowledgeable (and realistic) about the market, our resources and our competitors. We pursue the best we can reasonably afford . . . and accept that as a limit.

What I believe that most collectors do, although I have never seen this process discussed, is develop their own "sliding scale" of rating a piece from *1* to *10* based on what is important to them, what they appreciate and like the most about any genre. In other words, they develop and refine their tastes. Our personal preferences remain grounded in established and personal criteria. How do collectors decide what they like the most? Let us look at a few examples of what I am talking about in hopes of delineating the desirable characteristics in a piece of Americana.

Using Style and Connoisseurship Criteria

In 1999, a book was published, *Evaluating Your Collection: The 14 Points of Connoisseurship*, compiled by Dwight Lanmon as part of the *Winterthur Decorative Arts Series*. He dedicated the tome to Charles Montgomery, whose collecting criteria had previously appeared in a little known and less-read 1961 work: *The Walpole Society Note Book* and in his book, *A History of American Pewter* (1973). A leading expert in American decorative arts, Montgomery held the directorship at the Henry Francis du Pont Winterthur Museum. His central revelation is that the design elements of objects do not exist in isolation. For instance, Queen Anne pad feet on a chair or a table relate to a particular period, taste or style. An eagle weathervane from the 1870s and the inlaid eagle on a piece of 1790 furniture each may reflect differing periods of history and unique ideas of patriotism. Wonderfully, Lanmon teaches us not to mistake informed, refined taste for elitism. The first example of collectibles in his book when talking about condition is a Honus Wagner (Pittsburgh Pirates) baseball card! Each chapter in my previous book *Come Collect with Me* features an item features an antique my wife and I own and discusses it using Lammon's criteria. Not all are *10s*; that is the point.

What are Lanmon's criteria for understanding, talking about, and judging an antique's style?

- *Overall appearance* (useful when comparing two examples. Does what the craftsman or artist tried to do actually work?)
- *Form* (an object's outline, border, angles, curves. Short or tall, is it in proportion. sturdy or delicate?)
- *Ornament* (Decorative traits)
- *Materials* (what is the object made of?)
- *Finish* (original or aged, rough or smooth)
- *Period* (when made?)
- *Color* (muted, vivid, intense)
- *Craft techniques* (quality, how constructed, uniqueness)
- *Trade practices* (part of a set, labeled)
- *Function* (What the object was used for, why it was made?)
- *Style* (how the visual features combine. A summary judgment of the piece)
- *Attribution* (signed, stamped, by a known hand, forgery)

- *History of the object and its ownership* (documented)
- *Condition* (wear and tear where one would expect, originality, softening, aging)
- *Evaluation* (A collector's overall assessment of the object. Is it beautiful to you? Is it worthy of purchase and at what price? Your preference.)

For those readers counting the criteria, yes, 15 are listed. Lanmon presents "finish" as one of the 14. Montgomery in his book on pewter presents "date" and omits "finish."

Frankly, I do not believe most collectors consciously work their way through a list such as this when they see a piece. Instead, over time collectors develop a sense that many, most or all of these qualities contribute to the worth of an object and, at the same time, understand that for them there are some few that make an antique personally appealing and worthy of pursuit. You recognize disparate individual values at work at an auction when, say, an item of furniture far exceeds its estimate. Oftentimes what has taken place is that two or more bidders have done their homework and made an attribution as to who the craftsman was or that the piece, while not attributable to a specific craftsman, was probably made at his workshop. It is "in the school of." This style criterion is not terribly important to me but to some collectors it is the Holy Grail. They lust after such pieces. Even if the table has been refinished or it is larger than is typically thought of as "excellent," attribution trumps all the other connoisseurship criteria and its price soars.

Somehow, I managed to reach an inflection point in collecting. High country furniture filled the house. Though I had been collecting for years, I suddenly realized I was instinctively applying a host of criteria and that I had developed my own rank order of desirability. What did I learn about myself and my collection? Scale and proportion, originality (but selectively applied), and minimal ornamentation where most important to me. Give me a drop front desk that is 36 inches wide (a very desirable proportion) that had been refinished, and one in original surface that was a bit wider, and I would choose the original surface. A highboy with all the bells and whistles, and affordable because it had been refinished, would be less interesting to me than one that was plainer but with origi-

Using Style and Connoisseurship Criteria

nal or a very old surface. A painted surface is appealing to me, but only in the plainer, New England style. I own no Pennsylvania blanket chests with unicorns, flowers, scroll work, and curlicues painted on them. My wife and I love a Pennsylvania blanket chest we own in original blue with muted salmon trim. I like a desk with a fan or two but have seen them with several interior fans which is too much for me and unappealing. Other collectors would moan, "What is wrong with you?"

What it comes down to is that I will sacrifice some desirable traits if the piece has great scale and surface. Replaced brasses if appropriate are acceptable to me, though there are purists who would blanch at the thought. Hence, I own a highboy with several replaced brasses that are later 18th century, the originals are earlier, and even a chest of drawers with accurate Ball and Ball reproduction brasses. The chest is so very good in other ways. Replaced hinges on a drop front desk (someone forgot to pull out the lopers and the lid was unsupported and broke off) do not cause me to reject the antique. No, none of these items is perfect. None meets all the criteria so painfully listed for consideration. Being both a realist and somewhat less than wealthy, I settle for what makes me feel good about what I collect rather than whining about what I find minor imperfections. I have created my own list of criteria and apply them in pursuing antiques to own. And that is precisely what almost all collectors do.

I apply differing criteria to the redware I collect, of course. I saw a dish that was most affordable, with "Mary's dish" fired on it in slip, but its condition did not meet my standards and I passed on it. I will wait to buy hope another, nicer example hits the market Rim chips bother me if numerous and large, but I learned repairing a piece of redware is affordable and at the level I am collecting probably does not affect value. So, if I most desirable piece became available and I loved it aside from its chips, I would probably have it restored. I like smaller round plates and those in an oval shape but not large round platters. I can give you no reason for the latter. It is more an issue of what appeals to me as an individual,

The only criterion that Montgomery omits I would add is "sentimental value" that I discuss in Chapter 8. My wife and I have held onto several pieces we probably should have upgraded but because of the stories associated with them, or the fact our young children sat at the table, or

Lessons (Sometimes Waiting to be Learned)

we purchased them from dear friends, we held onto them. In other words, there are times that the criteria are thrown out the window for other considerations.

I wish *Good, Better, Best* books existed for genres other than furniture. I would love a book on weathervanes that shows the same vane with minimal wear with the gesso showing, one weathered with a great patina, one painted, and perhaps a fourth with repairs. The same vane could be shown in different sizes as well. Such a display would help me (and I assume other collectors) develop our style and connoisseurship preferences for this genre in a relatively short amount of time.

What it all boils down to is that all is not lost when a collector develops his eye, even when he knows to be the best is beyond his financial means. What a collector does is purchase items that he will be most happy living with, that have the style and connoisseurship design elements most important to him. In my small but growing collection of redware is a plate with a rim chip or two larger than I typically want. But the dish reads, *Sarah's Dish* and Sarah was my mother's name so sentimentality and the fact it made me smile eclipsed condition. If one enters the market in better condition, I will be interested in it, and I can always broker the one I already own.

I believe that most collectors can learn to appreciate what makes a piece of furniture, painting, clock, pewter, or quilt *Good, Better or Best*. As I wrote in *Come Collect with Me*:

> If someone like me – who my wife will tell you has no real sense of fashion, cannot dance worth a dang (don't feel the music), and does not have much of a sense of how best to arrange, display, and decorate our home – at this point in my life can identify and assess wonderful American antiques, then connoisseurship is surely within your grasp as well.

No matter what you collect, a collector must master style and connoisseurship criteria.

Chapter 30

The Virtues of Patience

Remember the wisdom granny taught you. He who hesitates is lost, Strike while the iron is hot and Look before you leap. Rushing pell-mell into purchasing antiques can be fatal. On the other hand, nothing drives serious collectors and dealers crazy as the person who looks and looks, hesitates, equivocates, delays, and never buys anything.

My concern is that there are merits on both side of the issue. Be cautious. Be decisive. How can that be? Jonathan Clements' *How to Think About Money* (2016) urges us to avoid being too focused on the short-term. Sometimes the urge to add to one's collection, fill a spot in your home or shelf or cupboard of antiques, or to be in the game is quite strong. Antique collectors building nice collections need to learn – or already have – that sometimes the most fulfilling antique shows, visits to dealers' shops, or auctions are ones in which they purchase nothing. Buying nothing leaves money in your pocket for the next time and means you have demonstrated self-discipline. Focus on what is on your wish list, specific items and their quality. Keep in mind that you may encounter an antique not on your list that takes your breath away, an "I have to own that and want to live with it forever" moment. Clements writes exhaustively how having a nice-sized nest egg for retirement is a decades' long process. The same holds true for building an antique collection. It seems appropriate that we should ponder the patience collectors must nurture as they go about amassing treasures they first covet and then cherish.

First, let us define our terms. Patience is the ability to abide delay, frustration, and trouble with equanimity. Flying commercially comes to mind. One enters a Zen-like state, knowing that the process of getting from point A to Point B is largely out of one's control. The runway is under the command of the tower. The plane is under command of the pilot. The weather . . . forget it. All you can do is sit back, sip your five-buck Bud Lite and be transported. No sense being upset by unexpected events. No relief in feeling depressed or victimized. Patience can be little more than despair wearing the cloak of virtue.

Undoubtedly, we all wish to be virtuous, even if it is compensatory. Waiting, patience, the refusal to be pushed precipitately, hesitation can all be good things. Dilatoriness, indecisiveness and denial of good impulses can be bad. The trick is to commit oneself to the side of the angels and avoid that of – dare I say it? – the dark side. Oh, and the real trick is telling the difference.

The Small Irritants That Truly Make Patience a Virtue

Collectors put up with a lot of nuisances. How is it most antique shows are in venues where the restrooms were last remodeled when Washington was president? I am thinking of the often absence of good food. I am thinking of the crippling chairs provided at auctions. (Are all those folks at the rear of the auction house surreptitiously talking on cell phones and bidding? Absolutely not. They are walking around and stretching so their back stays somewhat functional throughout a long day.) I am thinking of the rarity of small courtesies such as liquids for those waiting in line, shelter for those standing in the rain.

To be patient in these conditions requires looking for (and sometimes making up) positives. If the line for a show is long, talk with people waiting near you. You never know what great stories you will hear and what wisdom you will gain. It also makes the time go faster. Be prepared. To avoid numbing boredom, bring good coffee to an auction and something to read. At an outdoor show when the rains come, have that rain jacket handy. You get the idea.

Keep in mind that you are a patient collector. You know that "this too shall pass." In 10 hours, 10 days, or 10 weeks you will have forgotten the discomforts and indignities you experienced as a paying customer when you look at the piece you bought at that show or auction. And since you will re-experience such indignities time and time again, patience truly is a virtue. It will keep your blood pressure down and a smile on your face.

Be Patient with Yourself

Keep in mind that you are <u>choosing</u> to collect (although once at it a while it may feel more like a compulsion or addiction). You chose to book the 5:30 am flight to have a bit more time in New Hampshire. You chose to get to the show early and wait for hours. You chose to drive several hours to look at a piece a dealer called you about. You may begin to wonder if you are a bit crazy or question why you spend your time collecting. It is necessary to be patient with yourself, to acknowledge the highs you experience as an antique collector and to remind yourself that these positive outweigh the negatives. When they no longer do, it may be time to try another hobby.

Be Patient With Others

If I find an enticing treasure at auction about which I have questions, the sooner they are answered the sooner I know if this is an antique I will be bidding on. Still, most auction personnel are busy folks. My email inquiring about a piece or two at one of many auctions is not first on their priority list. At times their response can seem maddeningly slow. I have learned to keep a note on any piece I inquire about – auction date, auction number for the piece, brief description as a reminder to myself, and the date I first inquired. As the auction grows closer, and if I still have received no response I will call. Typically, I get the information I need in a timely manner but sometimes patience is called for.

The most difficult situation for me is when a dealer tells me he is visiting a collector or has heard about a piece I have coveted for some time. And then silence descends. I try to manage a situation like this by being upfront with the dealer, asking how long I should wait before I can be in contact about the antique in question. That way I know I have a set deadline for my patience.

Stepping Back and Taking Time Off

The psychological phenomenon that I describe in Chapter 16 (The Frenzy for Fresh to the Market) is relevant to our understanding of collector patience. It describes the fact that we no longer sense (see, smell, hear, etc.) any stimuli to which we are repeatedly exposed. For example, if you work in a shop that plays music all day, after a while you no longer hear it. Habituation is a phenomenon antique collectors must be aware of.

If you are a dedicated collector who gets alerts from multiple websites on a daily basis, goes to show after show or auction after auction, reads several antique publications a week – in other words, lives and breathes your hobby – what happens is that your eyes glaze over and you cease to be able to process, see, discern, or even notice what it is you are supposed to be paying such close attention to. Patience is necessary. Take a few days off. Go for a walk and smell the roses or watch for the presence of saber-toothed predators. Take a sabbatical from collecting for a few weeks, perhaps longer. Reinvigorate yourself. When you return to antiques, the entire antique world will seem fresher, more nuanced, and you will feel alive once again. You will notice things.

Be Patient With the Cussedness of Things

Collectors habitually rant about how their beloved possessions "talk to them." As a matter of fact, antiques are notable for their dumbness. Chips, dirt, sticky drawers and hundreds of other condition issues are the aphasia of the ancient. What an enthusiastic and knowledgeable collector perceives as patina may be little more to the impatient tyro than rust or inkblots. Every collector should be familiar with the insight of John Milton, who wrote in *Paradise Lost*, "They also serve who only stand and wait." Give things time. Let them find their voice in your heart. It is not unusual to find antiquarians who began their accumulations committed to one narrow category – weathervanes or redware. Yet over time their passion widens and gains depth. This is the most difficult and rewarding virtue you can attain.

Think of Building a Collection as a Marathon

If you catch the collecting bug, you are going to be at it for a while – a few years, often longer. The notion that one should buy the best one can afford rings true for many. Patience becomes apparent in several ways. You may not know what makes you smile until you have been collecting for some years. You will figure it out. Saving money to fund your collection also takes time. Of course, if a piece you must own enters the market you can try to pay it off over time. While doing so, keep in mind you are precluded from purchasing other antiques. Try to be intentional about what your collecting costs now and what funds may be available to you in the years ahead. If you expect your income to increase over time, an inheritance (that uncle you never knew about who owned a million-acre sheep farm in Australia dies and names you as an heir) appears, other expenses decrease (your children all get full college scholarships – you love them, oh, so dearly), then in the future you should have more disposable income to allot towards buying antiques.

As a collector in your first decade or so of collecting, it will take time to find venues that have items that interest you. The same is true for finding dealers who are willing to work with you and can search for what you want. Nonetheless, if you never buy from a dealer who is assisting you, the relationship will not last long. You may see auctions advertised that seem to have pieces you might want but the auction house never returns calls or emails asking about condition. Either you will have to go in person, and that could mean travel costs and time, find someone to look at the item for you, or look elsewhere. It all takes time.

I have written before about what I labeled "the wait," that patience also means doing without. If there is a certain piece you want, it may take years before you are the proud collector who owns it. A good example is my search for a high country desk that was the best possible. I had grown used to the wait, so I was confident I was not going to buy an example for the sake of owning one. Living without is more than okay, it is mandatory if collectors are to build a collection that they are proud of. I had seen several high country desks at antiques week in Manchester/Concord that seemed contenders – until their lids were lowered, but the interiors were only so-so. After a long dry spell, a dealer sent me photos of a desk being downsized from a collection. What a beauty! Two fans, original surface, great form. The wait was worth it.

You cannot control who dies, gets divorced, or divests. You may be outbid on items at auction, be second person to put a hold on something at a show and lose out. The hammer may be about to go down at an auction and at a last second a new bidder enters, driving up the price beyond what you choose to pay. All you can do is shake your head, perhaps mutter an expletive deleted or two, and move on. You may be the late-to-enter bidder next time. It really is a marathon. The fun is in The Hunt. Keep telling yourself that.

Patience is a Currency in Antique Collecting

The truth is that patience is a virtue needed by all parties in the antique collecting world. Your spouse will have to be patient with you as you collect – the catalogs and piles of books, time spent at the computer, time away from home. Your children also have to live in a house with all that "old stuff." Their friends may feel sorry for them. "Can't your parents afford nice things?" Dealers will need patience with you – your questions, equivocating, asking for time to pay off that expensive thing, the "Have you found it yet?" query. Truly patience greases the antique collecting engine.

There are many payoffs for patience. You will be prepared. Your mental health may be better. And you will be ready to pounce and spend money. After all, the patience is a prelude to truly striking when the iron is hot. When that piece you have been looking for becomes available, it is time to buy. It is the moment to be decisive. Else, stand and wait with the angels. Self-control and avoiding a short-term view are lessons to walk on by. This self-restraint runs counter to American society's pressure to buy, buy a lot, and buy now. You may need some mantras to help you maintain self-control. "Not spending is magical and good," or "I can live without it, I really can." Often at shows I attend the antiques I love are beyond my financial means. By using self-control, I can accrue enough purchasing power to buy one every now and then. Self-control allows you to have a few items that are really good. The adage is "Buy the best you can afford." The trick is to define "afford" as once in a while, sometimes a great while.

Collectors need to hone their patience.

Section V

A Wish or Two and Ending With Praise

Chapter 31
An American Antique Critic

Reviews and critics dominate and on occasion irritate our existence. Most big city newspapers have or have had a restaurant critic, typically unknown to the restaurateurs, usually with the rapacity of a wolf, if not its taste buds. Automobiles – one of the largest purchases we make in our lifetimes – are endlessly analyzed online and in print. Artists, art shows, symphonies and sundry musical genres, theater, films, all fall to the alleged expertise, questionable tastes, and actual scrutiny of reviewers. To read the Sunday *New York Times* and skip its book reviews marks you as a Philistine or a Neanderthal.

Those who publish in the interests of collectors of Americana perform marvelously, and I read their magazines, gazettes, and journals regularly and closely. At the same time the print media devoted to American antiques are not large or wealthy enough to bite the proverbial hand that feeds them, so the peril inherent in a regular critic's column looms large. Ideally, were there to be a critic who published in these pieces, a firewall between the editor and the critic's column would be necessary. Such an ideal verges on the unimaginable. Independent (and assuredly, sometimes, negative) reviews would be too much a risk and a hassle. Ergo, we have no James Beard, the sainted food critic, to assess the American antique universe. A comment or two, grousing or incisive, on social media seems the extent of what is available.

A Wish or Two and Ending With Praise

An independent critic could counterbalance offerings by existing publications that celebrate the American antique market and community. Which is all well and good, but as a result we collectors confront press releases and reviews that recognize almost all shows and auctions as triumphs, even those that prove on examination (alas!) to have been less than stellar successes. Sweeping adjectives rule the day and insight, "journalism," if you will, is somewhat in short supply. As one dealer told me, "When the effort has been made to procure interviews, the assertions [one gives] are accepted . . . and never fact-checked, let alone pushed back upon." I do not deny the presence of competent journalists in the universe of American collectors, with expert insight sometimes present, but I believe a critical eye is needed.

Thus, an opportunity for an independent voice exists, a niche that if filled would be great fun. So, what are the considerations, the obfuscations, the barriers, the rules that would have to be examined?

The collecting industry seems large enough to justify the presence of such a person. I reached out to the editor of *Maine Antique Digest* and learned there are no hard numbers for the size of American antique transactions because Standard Industrial Classification codes (which I never knew existed) lump antiques (even the tony auction houses, one imagines) in with "Used Merchandise Stores" (oh the irony). Still, he felt my guess that the industry sees $100 million per year change hands was low. Despite the substantial fiscal size of its market the American antique community is more like a village than a metropolis. That hundred mil plus spreads across a population that has knowledge, experiences, gossip, and scandalous opinions in abundance. Oh, and they want every one of those categories refined, confirmed, denied, and conflated, which is just what a critic does. Readers abound.

My suggestion. I would do what reporters are doing nationwide. Take as an example my hometown, which – like so many – saw the local newspaper consumed by the Gannet empire, whose rag ignores just about everything from government to letters to the editor, to the school system. It sketches a world of advertisements, obituaries, the Green Bay Packers (the state religion) and high school sports. Period. In reaction, a retired journalism professor from the city's University of Wisconsin campus has started an online "newspaper," featuring real reporting, available for a fee to interested readers. He is not alone nationally, and the instance offers a model for the critic I propose. Therefore . . . such a critic would have an online presence, a website, blog, or podcast.

What, exactly, would an antiques-collecting critic need? The food critic's cred rests on his (or her) paunch, the dramaturgy assessor on her spats and cane and cape (well, at least in a bygone era), the art critic on his eye. But that's all superficial stuff. What a good critic needs – outside of irritability, skepticism, and a vocabulary – is contacts, a mental list of who to ask and whom to trust. And the critic must be willing to not only dig in, the way researchers do, but to get his/her hands filthy, the way anthropologists do.

The American Antique critic could do more than simply "review." He could be an observer and a commentator. Such a person could write about shows, exhibitions, auctions and private sales, even particular *objets* or talk about the same in podcasts. He could rate shows on material available (tired, fresh), aesthetics, prices asked, the need for different dealers or genres, even the comestibles available (see what I mean about needing vocabulary? Chow, in other words). Her column could look at auctions. Did grievous errors exist in item descriptions? Who got the best buy? What item seemed the most overpriced (gasp, an overpriced antique at auction?). It happens all the time.

A critic could talk about market trends perhaps in a quarterly "intelligence report." Are they stable or declining for the middle or top tier? Why and what does this movement indicate? How about a "year in review" piece, or "predictions on the year upcoming?" Using one of the free survey instruments available for online purposes, the site could gather data and disseminate results. Lots of publications have an "opinion" column, sometimes written by the same author and sometimes by a rotating group. Collectors and dealers can hardly be said to lack opinions, prejudices, grievances. Anyone who has indulged in conversation while waiting in line at a show can testify to that fact, and some are startlingly good (as well as laughably bad). What is absent is a forum where they can be lauded, corrected and – yes – exposed. Don't discount such opinion pieces as a source of interest, straightening out facts, providing an opportunity to wise advice or calling malefactors to account.

Were ours a perfect world, our critic would have to be fair and even-handed, unbiased as much as that is possible. But think of the last time a writer had the nerve to use the term "sloppy" in reference to Rembrandt. He must avoid moral righteousness and intellectual arrogance. Recall a moment when James Beard failed to criticize the denizens of some snooty restaurant as "louche." Superiority and entitlement are prerequisite for criticism. What is crucial is that the arrogance and bias is firmly rooted in personal competence. You do not become an authority simply by taking on the title. Above all else, a sense of humor helps both for the critic and the world he observes. The critic's purpose is to offer informed guidance, thoughtful opinion, education, advice, pleasurable banter, and now and then a well-deserved spanking. A good reviewer would question the canon. In so doing, he could bring and keep new collectors to the community as he educates, explains, and analyzes. More directly a *Tips for New Collectors* column published on occasion would make good reading.

Gossip can be fun and need not be malicious or injurious. What dealers scored a coup? Has the reviewer heard of a well-known auction house that is struggling? What was the story behind the bidding war for that antique sold last month that soared in price? Gossip sometimes teases and incites, but it often bares the truth.

Should our critic's website arise, how about a *Top Ten* column annually? Wouldn't it be fun to read about the criteria used in ranking auctions, food venues, rest rooms, extra-mile care for collectors, dealers' websites, catalogs, books, general writings, and more? Perhaps the most perplexing legal problems in coping with real and alleged American antiques could be presented in rank order: Ownership and authenticity disputes, dodgy valuations and access to expertise are not merely the source of allegations but often signal underlying and unresolved problems with our hobby (or should I say industry or passion?). Of course, you, the reader, would disagree with the criteria and the selections resulting in indignant but sometimes interesting letters to the critic. Again, all great and useful fun.

I would love this Voice of the Collector, this Lone Ranger of Antique Truth to remain anonymous. Many a past critic has been persuaded to wear a pseudonym as a disguise. Publius (employed by Alexander Hamilton, James Madison, and John Jay) is famously already taken, and *Ho Chi Minh* seems – uh – inappropriate. Maybe something like *Charon* (legendarily grumpy and the source of the old pun, "Charon, share a like") would work to fend off the offended. Clearly the critic would have to be part of the American antique scene in some capacity.

Am I nominating myself? I demur. I am too old and devoid of the necessary expertise. I do not know the American antique world and the people in the community well enough. Let us find someone younger with the requisite knowledge. Although I'd like to stick a fork in some of the blather-balloons and pretentiousness of the American antiques' community, I will leave such deflation to another. The pseudonymous critic may count on me subscribing to his efforts, however.

One more suggestion: I would love to read a "Dear Ann-Tiques" column. Collectors, dealers, and auctioneers could all write in, characterizing their woes and asking for advice on how to proceed. Perhaps your mother-in-law outbid you at auction or your second wife won't talk to your ex because your ex managed to get the antique tavern table in the divorce settlement that your current wife loves so dearly. What is one to do? Can the ex and current wife go to arbitration and work out custody care? Here a definite and prescriptive (not to mention intolerant) voice is badly needed to restore faith, virtue, and the American way.

I have said my piece. For any *Charons* in the American antique world, you know you have one supporter to begin with. Have you heard . . .?

The American antique community is vibrant and ever changing. There are stories waiting to be told.

Chapter 32

The American Antique Market

I was thinking of the parable of the blind men and the elephant that originated in an ancient Indian subcontinent about a group of sightless men who come upon an elephant, each feeling its body in a different place and then describing the animal based on their own experiences. The point is that we tend to describe our own absolute truth of matters based on limited subjective experience, while ignoring or diminishing other peoples' truths that may equally be based on their own subjective experiences.

Which got me thinking of the famous 1951 Japanese movie, *Rashomon*, that examines the nature of truth. Each of four people describe different versions of the rape of a woman and the murder of her husband. This search for truth lead to what now is called "the Rashomon effect" that encapsulates a situation that is described differently by different observers. It has led to research on how we think about, interpret, know, and remember what we experience – especially complex or ambiguous situations.

All of which is preface for what I want to talk about: assessing and describing the state of the marketplace for American antiques. I write a monthly blog (comecollectwithme.com) and in March 2020 I briefly explored the issue, wondering about the robustness of the marketplace for such antiques. I was prompted by the editorial in the March 2020 issue of *Maine Antique Digest, Riding a Tailwind*, citing January in New York and concluding that ". . . the market is continuing a steady trend upward . . ."

The social scientist in me wonders about more data and about "more nuance." as I called it. With few American antique dealers at the Winter Show and its enormous overhead costs (tens of thousands of dollars I have been told) what does it mean for any one of them to have a good show, and can we generalize from their experience to dealers showing elsewhere? More generally, what criteria do we use to assess the state of the marketplace, and can we even get valid data to do so? Hearing promoters quoted as saying the "gate was up," or that "sales were up, especially smalls" tells us nothing about money being made or lost. And back to *Rashomon*, whose perspectives do we use to draw our conclusions and how much weight do we give each? After all, New York in January seems to be the upper end of the market. Does success at that level even trickle down to shows and auctions with more affordable goods? And what is a successful auction anyway? – back to *Rashomon* I am afraid.

In the same issue of *MAD* an article notes there will be no St. Charles spring show (it is usually held in a Chicago suburb), in my mind one of the strongest shows in the Midwest for American antiques. And the article points out dealers had good sales at past shows. Was there no waiting list of dealers, or what happened? The cancelling of this show does not seem to be a "tailwind." Much below the rarified air of the Winter Show (which I have never attended but would love to do so, do not get me wrong) I know of at least one dealer, who has nice pieces, who barely made expenses at Nashville (several shows held in the same February week) in 2019. I hope he did better this year. Another dealer profiled his Nashville experience on Instagram and said he had no retail sales. His nice-looking booth displayed fine antiques at reasonable prices. Those are only two examples, and I am hesitant to draw conclusions from such a small sample but . . .

Let's start our description of the American marketplace (our metaphorical elephant) by looking at auction houses. What is a successful auction? I know this seems like a silly question but bear with me. Let us assume that an auction is held with no reserve and offers high-end pieces.

A Wish or Two and Ending With Praise

The percentage of items that sell is close to 100 percent. Some of the pieces bring six-figure prices. Yet the consignors lose money on many such pieces that they bought when the market was higher. They are not terribly dismayed, as they full well knew this outcome was possible, and they wanted to disperse their collection for a variety of reasons. From their perspective the auction was successful.

From the auction house's point of view the auction also was successful. It had "guaranteed" a base price for some pieces that sold to bidders, and the total auction proceeds brought in a nice profit. The auction house reputation was enhanced or reinforced. As a result, it is likely to get more such consignors in the future.

But what does the marketplace conclude? Prices were well below what they used to be for most pieces but higher than a few years ago. Is the market back, is the tailwind blowing strong? If the consignors had been disappointed with the results, would the cognoscenti have different interpretations? I suspect various players in the American antique world would interpret the same auction differently, depending on their place in this universe and their viewpoint of what transpired.

Before I enter the world of dealers, let me talk about the accuracy of data related to the buying and selling of American antiques. Rarely have I talked to a dealer, or read about one, who flat out says, "I had a terrible show." When asked how they did, they seemed to say, "Okay;" "I am waiting for follow-up from some customers, as often happens"; "I sold to some new customers" (never saying how many pieces or the profit made). After all, why appear to be failing, why be negative about the world one inhabits, why seem petulant, blaming the promoter or others? Dealers are quick and I assume honest when they talk about what they sold – a cupboard, some redware, two weathervanes, a partridge in a pear tree.

Sometimes they talk about buying well during setup or selling well during setup. But we do not know how many dollars a dealer is making. We would need that information to accurately assess the state of the marketplace. A lot of activity does not mean great profit, although it may. In other words, we may never know the state of the American antique marketplace. Dealers leaving before retirement age and for reasons unrelated to their health would be one clue, as would younger dealers entering the profession and doing it full time.

The assessment of the marketplace is shaded by the different business models of its dealers. Some sell full-time and must pay their health insurance and contribute to their IRAs or 401s from their profits. Others sell part-time and have a cushion of other income and fringe benefits to fall back on. Still others have deep pockets and can afford the slow times or not doing well because their financial resources allow them to do so. Whose perspective, even if we knew dealers' circumstances, would we use to assess the marketplace robustness? We are back to the elephant or *Rashomon* once again.

Other variables also come into play. How astute is the dealer, i.e., how good at his craft? We would expect a dealer who works hard, picks well, has a good eye, keeps in touch with his clients, has an up-to-date and full website, advertises wisely, and has loyal collectors in various locations where he shows (a girl in every port) to be successful. Such a dealer would manage his financial resources well, not buying for the sake of it, going in with other dealers perhaps for "special" pieces, and not holding such pieces forever if they fail to find a buyer. If such a dealer is struggling, that would be a more valid indicator of the state of the market than a dealer who lacks several of those characteristics. But dealers are not objectively typed. Fellow dealers and collectors form their impressions and conclusions, but it could be that there are more than a few dealers thought of as "lacking," who make a fine living. We do not know.

My preference for the type of dealer by which to assess the health of the American antique marketplace (and you may well have a different one) would be one who makes a living from the buying and selling of antiques and is dependent on his business for a living. Such a dealer may have an ownership in a group shop or an online venue to provide income, the latter being part of the marketplace in my mind. Looking at sellers who work in selling and buying American antiques as a full-time occupation, I worry about the marketplace when I hear of dealers struggling to make costs at good shows.

Another view of the marketplace is more objective. In looking at antique shows many are now "art and antique shows," "garden and antique

A Wish or Two and Ending With Praise

shows," or contain a wide variety of pieces, some mid-century modern or even newer. A different array of what is for sale is needed to attract customers and buyers than used to be the case. That is one sign to me that the marketplace may be struggling, or at the least, it certainly has changed.

Let's return to *Rashomon* and use my own collection as an example. If I live a long life (full disclosure, I am 75 years old), one free of dementia, I will consign my American antiques to one or more auction houses. At that point in my life, I would want them to do well financially but what "well" means to me might differ from another collector in the same situation. If I die or other physical health problems arise, one of my sons is executor of my estate. He would not want antiques returned so would care less about how well the items do financially at auction. His goal would be to disperse the items and close the estate. Depending on who you ask, he or me or the other collector, you very well may get different opinions about the market. Whose opinion do we use to assess how robust it is?

The group shop also enters the equation. What is a successful group shop? Is it one that makes money for its owners or one that dealers do well at? Cannot a group shop do well with only part-time dealers? Is the marketplace robust if dealers consign items to a group shop and let them sit? They are visible, there is a chance they will sell, but they are out of the way. Given the relatively few numbers of dealer shops with hours compared to yesteryear, the group shop must be factored into the marketplace. I do not know what criteria to use to do so.

And let's not forget promoters who probably really know how dealers at their shows are doing if they ever could say (perhaps anonymously).

What I propose is the Perlman Index. (If the list of the hotness of chili peppers is named the Scoville index, why not use my name?) This index would summarize an annual gathering of data to assess the state of the American antique market. Once established it could be used to weigh against past years to determine if the market is up, flat, or down. What would the Perlman Index (known by the involved as *pi*, unless they are square) contain? How about:

- A confidential assessment of ten top end shows, middle tier shows and "average" shows with data provided by a sampling of dealers

who respond anonymously. If a dealer fails to respond, he would be replaced by another.
- A confidential assessment of the same shows by their promoters who are asked to supply the size of the gate and an "impression" of how dealers did on an agreed upon scale.
- An assessment of those who consigned American antiques to top and middle end auction houses. Again, responses would be confidential as to how pieces fared.
- An assessment of auction houses themselves, from those responding anonymously for select auctions and looking at total revenue, including buyers' premium against estimates.
- An item analysis of select auctions by looking at total revenue from "past auction" data, percentage of pieces sold, and so forth.
- A count of number of antique shows cancelled and the number of new shows.
- A count of the number of new auction houses (not counting existing ones that merge).
- A count of dealers leaving the profession and why (e.g., retirement, health, could not make a living).
- An operational definition of "highest quality" (top end), the middle market, and the bottom market, and tracking how pieces in each market did at auction.

Of course, such data collection would take effort and would have to be assessed every year or two to improve its accuracy and usefulness. Perhaps even more important what weightings does one give to the various market elements that would go into the Perlman Index for the year. Such an index is doable, and the three major American stock market indices could be a useful exemplar (The Dow Jones, S&P, and NASDAQ Composite).

The state of the market is not limited to American antiques for collectors. Those who collect classic cars, coins, stamps, Star War memorabilia, or British silver teapots face the same questions. As a collector I have spent a long time in the American antique community. It would be interesting to know its relative health.

The true financial state of the American antique market would interest many.

Chapter 33

A Paean for American Antique Dealers

An author determines how to end his book. Some sum up, a denouement perhaps, an epilogue, others look to the future. It depends on the book's genre and the author's style and goals. I offer thanks and accolades to you the reader for making it this far in *The Collector's World*. I hope your journey has proven worthwhile.

I end with plaudits also to one group in the American antique community – its dealers: hard working entrepreneurs who live by their wits, knowledge, dedication, and sheer stubbornness. Without them, collectors would indeed be lost. What follows is my attempt to applaud American antique dealers for what they do. I hope you agree with my sentiments.

Sometime in the future. They were believed extinct, but N.E. (New England) Jones would have nothing of it. Unpaved back roads beckoned in rural Maine and New Hampshire, rumors were rife, sightings were rare, others were hoping to beat him to the treasure, byways proved dead-end trails, and advice turned out to be no more than false leads. But he found his man, finally, living in a shabby 20-year-old tri-level in suburbia – what better place to hide? Sometimes truth is stranger than fiction. The last of his species, the only living dealer in American antiques. Or more accurately, the only living person who used to deal in American antiques, for he had quit years before. Antique dealers were no more.

A Paean for American Antique Dealers

"If only people had cared," the former dealer told New England. "It would have made it easier to watch the profession dying out – what we worked so hard, vanishing." He shook his head grimly.

New England looked around. There wasn't an American antique in sight. "Too painful," the former dealer said. "Got to move on. If only people how shown some esteem for us and it." His voice like an 18th century tavern table that had seen better days – tired, warped, any pretense long faded. No more old-and-wonderful, just old.

The Present. Come, let us celebrate the dealer in American antiques. No rhymes, chorus, or poetry, but an exaltation nonetheless full of jubilation and respect for those who make collecting American antiques possible. Their prosperity, resourcefulness and knowledge are hard-earned. Let us extol their contributions to the American antique community.

Dealers have been under duress. The pandemic made both buying and selling difficult indeed. This, even though lots of goods clutter the marketplace, some from collectors who needed to find a way out of a hole they didn't dig. There are fewer collectors to attract, an aging collector cohort that stares at houses full. The market shows lower prices (for most pieces) than a decade ago. More work with less profit. We are being assaulted by online platforms, some dealers gripe. In response, a handful of dealers have melded a host of on big-time auction houses with their smaller regional ones, to have a larger role in the selling of Americana. Woe to the collector if greater numbers of dealers become marginalized. For no one offers the skills, guidance, and service a dealer does. 'Tis true.'

Hence, the fabled antique pickers/dealers need a pick-me-up, a note of respect, an ode to joy (if Beethoven will so allow). I sing to their relevance and importance, extending a vote of confidence in and appreciation for them all.

The work of an antique dealer is harder than you imagine, even when she loves what she does. The list of tasks is endless: hours on the road, finding pieces to purchase, buying and selling right, keeping in touch with collectors, advertising, mastering and using social media, photography, and repairing vehicles. The demands on patience, surely so.

But the burden, we must acknowledge, embraces something far more demanding. Oh, you should listen to dealers' stories sometimes about collectors, their sins, their foibles. I hear you say, "Of course not you or me – paradigms of virtue and we pay on time." Hmm.

Connoisseurship in ascertaining the merits and worth of an antique is a skill honed over years. Even when imperfect it must be good enough for a surviving dealer not to end up owning more items that captured his heart than he can sell to collectors, museums, and the like. Becoming knowledgeable demands the sort of scholarship encouraged and taught by bitter experience. We talk so casually of their having an "eye," as if that came with the occupation. In fact, it must be trained, slowly, patiently, and – for most – expensively. Dealers risk their own money, buying without knowing how long they will own a piece, or if the market will endorse their taste and bear the price that they hope to fetch for it. Will buyers learn how right they are? As one dealer told me, "A great deal of skill per dollar of profit." How true.

Dealers maintain an inventory. At times they carry pieces for others, representing them. Or they buy back wonderful pieces they sold long ago, just because they want a chance to sell something of excellence. How many of us have heard the line, "If you ever want to sell that piece, let me know."

Few acknowledge the degree to which antique buying and selling is a hardy capitalist game (need one remind you what the Nobel Prize for Economics was in 2020? Yes, auctions). The surviving dealer must master the art of buying for a price and selling for more, that or the "Out of Business" cloud darkens his day. Pickers, nurtured over the years or decades knock on his door (or used to), hoping their expertise is equal to the dealer's – and there is plentiful evidence that picking is not a sucker's game. Dealers walk the show floor before the doors open, making quick decisions, and they are not averse to a stroll through group shops looking at pieces with expertise and experience as their only weapons. They indulge in endless work and more than a few hazards, seeking antiques, often with a specific collector in mind. Why do they do all this? Without an inventory there is nothing to sell, no shekels to take in.

Speaking of money, dealers need to know the markets as well as they do their wallets. American antiques as a broad category are really many smaller fiefdoms, many a complex web (e.g., furniture, artwork, smalls) that challenge both imagination and expertise. They need to know what has sold, for how much and where (shows, dealer to collector from a shop, by bid at auction). If you price goods too high, they may languish. Price them too low and profit is lost (and you look like you do not know what you are doing). Markets are not stationary; a dealer needs to know their direction for each genre he buys and sells.

To top it off, serious dealers need courage. Let us call them "trend setters." These gutsy sorts appreciate and love some genre of antiques out of the mainstream. They set themselves the challenge of creating a market for their wares. They need to educate potential buyers, make them knowledgeable, help them appreciate the aesthetic. The dealer thinks we should cherish the items he just knows are worth interest and affection. Dealers who take risks need an abundance of faith . . . and a full wallet.

Above all, to be a dealer in American antiques, you need to know and love history in all its dimensions. Dates are important, certainly, but insights into craftsmanship and how people lived are critical. Not just American history either, for many native pieces are intellectually married to roots in Europe. Speaking as a collector, I still find myself trying to delve into the origins and aesthetics of pieces in my home made before the American Revolution. A good dealer must be full of that learning, willing to share it, and open to guiding us amateurs into an understanding of what we have and what we are preserving. The antique dealer is often the bridge between things and enlightenment.

By now you have gathered that a dealer's core task is to instill a sense of delight and wonderment in collectors. Aesthetic appreciation is often diminished as mere feeling of love and awe for a great piece of Americana. Aesthetic appreciation goes well beyond intellectual acknowledgement and seriously impinges on emotional involvement with the object. We redefine an object as admirable when its qualities overwhelm us and takes our breath away.

How does a dealer become this guide? It is as much a learning process as any school education. A range of exemplars are displayed, assessed, and discussed with fellow collectors and other dealers. Books and periodicals are considered, and the antiques in them evaluated. But a depth of appreciation involves more than mere skill in identifying good examples. In time, an emotional involvement needs to grow. When it has, it is easy to identify. The dealer communicates his excitement in his tone of voice, his astonishment. Her loving caresses over the surface of a piece of furniture or her handling of a painting send a message to the buyer. This antique is IT, the real thing, desirable, marvelous. "Come," it shouts, "let us give thanks for that nameless (oftentimes) workman from so long ago and the fruits of his labor."

Not everyone who spends time at dealers' shops or antique shows comes to appreciate American antiques. The historic appreciation can be learned, but the calculus of developing an aesthetic appreciation is still somewhat unclear. Nonetheless, some folks become "collectors of American antiques" with all that the label entails, finding beauty in certain objects for their artistry and giving them value because of the magnificence they see in them. These collectors need dealers.

We (collectors) lean on dealers, too. "Did you see the piece coming up at auction?" "At Winterthur, Historic Deerfield, the latest exhibit at Colonial Williamsburg, the American Folk Art Museum, did you see . . .?" We are inexorably pushed towards, first, appreciation and then acquisition. The aesthetics of an antique becomes a goal, the collector the dealer's instrument. And the satisfaction arising from success in acquiring an antique we desire is what leads to the growth of the passion. Wanting, knowing, getting becomes a circle and at the center lies our delight and the dealers with whom we work. Think of the latter, that I, as a collector, could possible own this antique as "meta-awe," central to collecting. Isn't that what The Hunt is all about, that somehow, someday, the antique of my dreams will be mine?

As is true of any emotional response, this first kind of amazement and astonishment of having your breath taken away, is learned over time. Often it is borrowed, at least for a while, from someone who sees more deeply, has a greater command of context, understands how others will react to the antique. And that person is frequently the dealer.

Dealers develop in others the collector's "eye." Somewhat mystical, famous collectors are said to have it. Beyond financial acuity or the intellectual knowledge of American antiques, the "eye" is like an ear for music. Good antiques beckon and whisper to such collectors or dealers, "Come hither."

A Paean for American Antique Dealers

It is dealers, therefore who help us refine our tastes. But a multiplicity of forces is at work, not excluding individual tendencies. That is one reason collections vary so broadly. For my wife and me our passion turned out to be high country. Within that genre dwell individual pieces with original finish, paint, a rural heritage, and a smaller scale (the house is not that large); tallcase clocks; Hudson Valley paintings and portraits among others. We could not identify these as objects of beauty when we first started collecting, but that is where we (and our hearts) are now.

Are there others who can work with and educate collectors the way dealers do? I think not, especially for collectors early in their colleting lives. Shirley Mueller, author of *Inside the Head of a Collector* and lover and collector of Chinese export porcelain, believes that dealers are superior to museum curators in their knowledge. Whether you agree or not, some dealers truly are scholars, who authenticate and evaluate, providing a solid backstop for the collector. More than a few have hosted online educational videos about antiques in their inventory, authored pieces in national publications, or written highly researched blogs. Their scholarship shines through.

Dealers also are fellow travelers with us on our journey. Most dealers experience rich satisfaction watching us build our collections. They are our confidants, advisors, shaking their heads "no" or "yes" after looking at an item. They know who has what and when it may reach the marketplace. They suggest we go into debt for some pieces and offer an occasional, "If I were you."

Let us hope that dealers in American antiques prosper so that New England Jones never journeys abroad looking for the last of the breed. For dealers are too important to collectors to disappear. Their knowledge and relationships are the warp and weft of collecting American antiques, providing the fabric of our collecting community. With glasses raised high as we give homage to the humble antique dealer.

In celebrating them, Shelley comes to mind. "I have drunken deep of joy, And I will taste no other wine tonight."

As noted, the antique dealer is often the bridge between things and enlightenment.

Index

aesthetic appreciation, 122; dealers, 207-208

anticipation, 1-6; as problem solving, 3-5; created within us by others, 5-6; definition, 1-2; key to collecting, 4; motivates, 5

auctions, 135-140; collectors' beliefs, 138-139; competition, 139; emotion, 139-140; endowment effect, 139; halo effect, 139; house goal, 135-136; marketing, 136-138; pleasing others, 140; scarcity, 140; social proof, 140. See Timed auction

Babbidge, J., 64

bad behavior, collectors. See Collector sins and loss of virtue

Bachelder Battle of Gettysburg, 17, 89, 128

Bacon, R., 37

Baker, E., 64

Ball, G., 33

Barnum, P. T., 54

Beard, J., 193

Bishop, R., 61

Brown, R. M., 122

Browning, R., 179

buying, 167-172; buyer's remorse, 167-170; drought, 170-171; non-buyer's remorse, 171-172

Clements, J., 185

choice, 141-146; ceasing to collect, 142-143; changing genres, 142-143; freedom to choose, 143-145; know thyself, 145-146; no one path, 143

collection divestiture, 93-98; angst causing, 94; antique advisors, 97-98; being remembered, 98; ethical will, 97; problems, 94-96; solutions, 94-98

collections, living with or put away, 161-166; collector differences, 164; collector similarities, 162-163; need to see the collection, 163

collector sins and loss of virtue, 81-87; anger, 85-86; envy, 86; gluttony, 84; greed, 86-87; lust, 84; pride, 83-84; sloth, 85; treachery, 82-83

Index

collectors' angst. See Collection divestiture

color, 59-65; importance, 60; preferences, 60, 65; show booths, 75

concerns, 7-13; being deceived, 8; buying when one should not have, 11-12; caretaking, 13; mistakes, 11; paying too much, 8; trust, 10. See also Buying

condition, 66-72; collector differences, 67, 71; material culture, 67; passion versus comfort, 70; rarity, 69-70

connoisseurship, 179-184; dealers, 206

Conrad, J., 149

courage, 14-20; admitting mistakes, 19; dealers, 17-18, 207; definition, 14-15; doing what is right, 18; of one's convictions, 15-17

critic, American antiques, 193-197; attributes, 195-196; going about it, 194-196; independent journalism, 194

Dickenson, E., 27

disappointment, 21-26, 31; as a trait, 23-24; decision analysis, 24; definition 22-23; minimizing, 24; paradox of 23, 25-26; positive uses, 25-26; stress, 24

Dostoevsky, F., 27

Ecclesiastes 3:1, 93

Einstein, A., 129

Elliott, E. A., 64

existential collecting question, 25

faith. See Trust

Fales, D. A., 61

fresh to the market, 99-104; competitiveness, 100-101; conformity, 101; definition unclear, 99-100; desirability, 101-103; fallacy, 104; others' validation, 103; stories, 100

fulfillment, 117-122; definition, 119; example, 119-121

happiness, 117-122; definition, 118-119; example, 119-120

Hemingway, E., 56

history and American antiques, 89-92; bringing history to life, 89-92; dealers' love, 207; promoting our nation's past, 90; remembering history, 89-90

Index

hope, 27-32; definition, 28; desire, 29; dreaming, 31; encourages, 29; maintaining, 30-31; motivational system, 32; sustains collectors, 29; versus wishing, 30

Hubener, G., 62

Hunt, The, 2, 27-29; 31, 162, 166

Isley Brothers, 141

Klee, P., 59

Lammon, D., 181

Leonardo da Vinci, 66, 105

market, American antiques, 198-203; economic state is unknown, 198-199; measuring, 199-203; more data needed, 199; Perlman Index, 202-203

marketing, 147-151; buyer beware, 152; collector mistakes, 147-148; halo effect, 150; language is powerful, 148-151; noise, 148-153; word important as an example, 149-151

Miller, Jim and Bernice, 47, 120

Milne, A. A., 1

Milton, J., 188

mine, 105-110; ethics, 108; ownership is unclear, 105, 108

Montgomery, C., 181

Mueller, S., 209

Munch, E., 65

nostalgia, 33-39; characters, 37; definition, 33, examples, 34; here and now, 37; may hinder collectors, 34, 38; motivates, 34

Occam's Razor. See Fulfillment, happiness

paean to dealers, 204-209; aesthetic appreciation, 207-208; burdens, 205-206; connoisseurship, 206; courage, 207; guide, nurture and develop collectors, 207-209; hard work, 205-206; irreplaceable, 205; know the market, 206-207; love history, 207; scholars, 209

Pan Am Clipper, 24, 130-131, 152

pandemic, missing simple pleasures, 111-116; being with others, 112-113; dealers' shops, 115-116; in-person shows, 113-115; sense of touch, 114

Index

passion, 15, 40-45; case example, 43; definition, 40-41; formation, 43-44; harmonious, 42; losing, 44-45, 70-71; motivation, 42-43; obsessive, 42; self-defined, 41; well-being, 42

patience, 185-191; as a virtue, 190; collection building-marketing, 189-190; definition, 186; small irritants, 186-187; stepping back, 188; with oneself, 187; with others, 187-188

Pennington, C., 130

people, importance in collecting, 4-5. See also Notes on a pandemic

Porter, R., 64

preparation, 154-160; know the market, 157-159; market description, 154-157; tastes and wants, 158-160

Proust, M., 34

Roosevelt, E., 119

Sack, A., 68, 179

Salvator Mundi, 66, 105

Santayana, G., 89

Satre, J-P., 142

sentimentality, 46-51; definition and examples, 47; preserves innocence, 50-51; remembering, 47-49; selective, 50

Shakespeare, W., 31

Shelley, P. B., 209

show booth, well designed, 73-80; branding, 78; dealer cost and target revenue, 79; dealer tastes, 79-80; display and merchandising, 73-80; display cases, 75-76, 77; inventory, 79; sales environment, 74; view from without, 75; visual merchandising, 74-75; within the booth, 76

Stedman, A., 61-62

Smith, G., 130

Stillinger, E., 35

stories, 100, 183

style and connoisseurship, 179-184; criteria, 181-182; good pieces exceed budget, 179-180; pursuing the best a collector can afford, 180-184

Thoreau, H. D., 26

Index

timed auction, 173-178; bidding, 174-177; competitive, 175; description, 173-174; emotion and irrationality,175; last few minutes, 177; reserves, 174-175

too much stuff, 123-128; example, 123-124; problem, 124; solutions, 124-128; storing excess pieces, 127

top sellers, 128-133; behavioral economics, 132; expensive and wonderful, 133; fascination with, 129-132; gossip, 132-133

trust, 52-57, 95; auction houses, 54; dealers, 54; definition 53; difficult to give up, 54; gold standard in collecting, 57; hard won, 53; painful if violated, 53; risks, 56

weathervanes, 10, 16, 69

Wilde, O., 48

Wilder, T., 111

wisdom, collecting, xviii-xix

About the Author

Baron Perlman is a long-time collector of American decorative arts. His childhood and teen focus on stamps, comic books, and baseball cards was supplanted by American antiques. He was born to collect.

Born in Chicago Perlman attended Lawrence University (Appleton, WI) and then Michigan State University where he earned his master's and doctorate in clinical psychology. He served in the U.S. Army, including a tour in Vietnam.

Most of his professional life was spent in the Department of Psychology at the University of Wisconsin Oshkosh and in consulting. His applied work as a clinical psychologist including just plain listening and trying to "make sense of" serves him well as a collector. He is now joyfully retired.

His interests in collecting and writing have led to numerous columns that continue to be published in *Maine Antique Digest*. In 2019 he published *Come Collect with Me – Musings on Collecting and American Antiques*.

Married 50 years, his wife Sandy joins him in collecting. They have lived in Oshkosh, Wisconsin for a long time and have two sons and two cats. Neither son is as consumed with collecting as their dad is. Nor are the cats.

www.ingramcontent.com/pod-product-compliance
Lightning Source LLC
Chambersburg PA
CBHW030517080526
44586CB00011B/224